MW00898342

IN HINDSIGHT: FROM DENIAL to CLARITY

The Gifts of a Terminal Diagnosis

MAUREEN TONGE

with Kirsten Tonge

BALBOA.PRESS

A DIVISION OF HAY HOUSE

Copyright © 2020 Maureen Tonge with Kirsten Tonge.

All rights reserved. No part of this book may be used or reproduced by any means, graphic, electronic, or mechanical, including photocopying, recording, taping or by any information storage retrieval system without the written permission of the author except in the case of brief quotations embodied in critical articles and reviews.

This book is a work of non-fiction. Unless otherwise noted, the author and the publisher make no explicit guarantees as to the accuracy of the information contained in this book and in some cases, names of people and places have been altered to protect their privacy.

Balboa Press books may be ordered through booksellers or by contacting:

Balboa Press
A Division of Hay House
1663 Liberty Drive
Bloomington, IN 47403
www.balboapress.com
844-682-1282

Because of the dynamic nature of the Internet, any web addresses or links contained in this book may have changed since publication and may no longer be valid. The views expressed in this work are solely those of the author and do not necessarily reflect the views of the publisher, and the publisher hereby disclaims any responsibility for them.

The author of this book does not dispense medical advice or prescribe the use of any technique as a form of treatment for physical, emotional, or medical problems without the advice of a physician, either directly or indirectly. The intent of the author is only to offer information of a general nature to help you in your quest for emotional and spiritual well-being. In the event you use any of the information in this book for yourself, which is your constitutional right, the author and the publisher assume no responsibility for your actions.

Any people depicted in stock imagery provided by Getty Images are models, and such images are being used for illustrative purposes only. Certain stock imagery © Getty Images.

Print information available on the last page.

ISBN: 978-1-9822-5772-9 (sc)
ISBN: 978-1-9822-5773-6 (e)

Balboa Press rev. date: 11/04/2020

Contents

Acknowledgements

THIS BOOK IS a result of being the recipient of unconditional love and support of hundreds of friends, family – even strangers, from around the globe. Without the support of so many – whether it was a card, thoughtful gift, prayers, the GoFundMe account that helped bring my immediate family together more than once in the thick of my healing journey; or fundraisers hosted to support the Brain Tumour Foundation of both Canada and America it was all so very much appreciated and very humbling.

To my incredibly strong parents, Ray and Diane Tonge, who received the shock of their life when one of their four beloved daughters received a terrifying diagnosis of an inoperable Grade IV Glioblastoma multiforme, you define for me the term resiliency. I look up to you as role models and am particularly grateful I come from such hardy stock!

To my beloved twinnie, Kirsten Tonge, you remain the Yang to my Yin. We are meant to be together for decades to come. My advocate extraordinaire, your courage to ask the tough questions and use your experience in the field of medical insurance claims was invaluable. I treasure you.

To my younger sisters, Jocelyn Smith and Melanie McClelland, your faith in me despite your fears was so needed. Thank you for your humour and the gut-busting laughter we shared in person and more recently through video Messenger calls. There is no one I laugh more emphatically with than you two!

I am blessed to have an amazingly present extended family that I lovingly refer to as the Castor Clan, despite two of the Charpentier siblings not living in Castor. My deep connection with them is thanks to the unconditional love and support of the rock in my life: my husband,

Robert Charpentier. I cannot imagine having travelled this healing journey of mine without your unquestioning support. I adore you with every fibre of my being.

To my besties, Natalie Sweet and Lisa Yang, I'm quite certain no three individuals could be more different and yet love each other as much. Who knew that a small-town New Brunswick friendship that began in grade five and seven would last as many decades as it has?

Debbie Meade, your willingness to be with me at a moment's notice did not go unnoticed. I treasure our friendship, born almost twenty years ago in our adopted home of Yellowknife, Northwest Territories. You have been a beloved friend and we consider you and your two amazing girls like family. We love you.

Jillian MacKay, I credit you with allowing me to peel away the layers so that I could heal energetically, mentally, emotionally, and spiritually. It was an experience that defies words and I thank you for sharing your immeasurable and multi-dimensional gifts. I am a better and more whole person because of my work with you.

Though it's unlikely I'll return to the world of teaching high school, I'd like to acknowledge with much love the support of my Yellowknife Education District #1 family and most particularly the very special team at Ecole Sir John Franklin High School. You will always be a part of my life and I'm thrilled to have left a legacy with the "Leaving a Legacy Portrait Project". A special thank you to the admin team who was never anything but 100% supportive.

My Yellowknife friends who have become family over my 28 years of calling this city my home, I love and appreciate you dearly. My past students at Sir John, and all those who have supported me at Collective Soul Space, thank you for your ongoing loving gifts of friendship. Toni Riley, dear friend and cancer survivor, thank you for the idea of my "henna crown".

To NWT Arts for your generous grant to support the writing of my memoir. Specifically, I'd like to acknowledge the love and letters of support I received for my grant application from Johanna Tiemessen and Nancy Mullick, fellow souls at Collective Soul Space.

There are truly too many friends outside of the NWT to list everyone who gifted me with opportunities to grow and learn in my yoga teacher training and practice, along with their love and support through this journey. Devinder Kaur, Dev Suroop Kaur, Khomal Bhasin, I love you. Erin Sproule, my younger soul sister, you have brought me joy in your joy. My dear extended family and friends who continue to support me across the country, I can't express my gratitude deeply enough. Although physically distant, the very special group in the Class of '86 forming lifelong friendships and loving support during my journey – thank you seems inadequate. Barry and Mary Beth Tonge and Jo and Jeff Granberg, thank you for opening your Edmonton homes and your loving support of our family when it was needed.

To the medical team at Cross Cancer Institute in Edmonton, Alberta, thank you for your perpetual compassion and care; I have been in great hands! Specifically, I would like to acknowledge the kindness, compassion and patience of Dr. Easaw and his team for all of their dedication and encouragement.

My integrative team consisting of the brilliant and incredibly kind Dr. Shahin Moslehi in Yellowknife, his mentor Dr. Paul S. Anderson, co-author of *Outside the Box Cancer Therapies*, who virtually consulted with Sha for free, recommending a protocol for me to follow, Dr. Erik Boudreau from the Fort Langley Integrated Clinic in British Columbia who was integral in crafting my integrative protocol and Dr. Brent Barlow out of Kelowna, BC who was the first to recommend that I find an integrative specialist in Fort Langley. Not once have I ever felt alone on this healing journey of mine. I acknowledge my local family doctor, Marlies Houwing as well for ensuring I got all of the blood work done on time and for her wonderful caring and genuine compassion when I was initially diagnosed and then experienced the setback.

Sukdev Jackson, thank you for honouring me with loving permission for my use of Aykanna's beautiful music, and to Beautiful Chorus for the Hymn of Healing that made it to my BT Playlist and permission to cite in my memoir.

To my editor, Kimmy Beach, thank you for having taken a chance of a complete rookie in the world of authorship. Your willingness to place your trust in me is so very much appreciated. I look forward to sharing the end result with you.

Prologue

BY THE END of 2018, it was becoming readily apparent to me, but also to those to whom I'm closest, that all was not right in my world. I was struggling with exhaustion as a result of insomnia. I suffered from anxiety and was, by all accounts, depressed. My senses had gone into overdrive. Specifically, scents and sounds would drive me into an unreasonable and almost uncontrollable rage. My poor husband bore the brunt of my anger, as I would explode at him for the overwhelming stench of his "chemical-filled" body wash/shampoo. I accused him of using it on purpose to make me feel ill! (Note: once I started healing, I could barely smell the same body wash/shampoo.) And his snoring! Despite my early Christmas gift of Bose Sleepbuds, I could still hear his snoring. To make matters worse, I was becoming incontinent. I found a way to explain my symptoms that I'd begun to experience: I'd written them off to coming from a long line of Henderson/Alexander women who struggled with bladder control. Particularly when one has a "to-do" list a mile long and just wants to check off one more item before relieving oneself: or laughing so hard that, well, I leak. I certainly didn't believe anything I was experiencing was neurological; I was far too healthy for that.

That said, I felt entirely unbalanced, which was hard to admit, seeing that, as a yoga instructor, and a huge fan of kayaking, I had made my entire life about finding balance. There were times I thought I was becoming unhinged. I am certain that my husband did too. This book is an openly vulnerable recounting of my journey back to health, from being in utter denial to taking full accountability.

Chapter 1

In Denial

I AM LIVING—IN FACT thriving—with a brain tumour. In late February 2019, I received the diagnosis of a brain tumour, but not just any brain tumour. A biopsy confirmed that it was one of the most highly aggressive types of tumours out there: the same that felled The Tragically Hip's front man, Gord Downie, and Senator John McCain: an inoperable grade IV Glioblastoma Multiforme. According to the neurosurgeon, I was given four months to less than a year. He did not believe I would make it to the end of 2019. I'd declined to hear my prognosis when it was initially delivered to my sis and husband by the neurosurgeon. It wasn't until December of 2019, when my sister figured there was no question of my not surviving the earlier prognoses, that she revealed the original timeline. My initial information a few months into my healing journey detailed fourteen to sixteen months if I was lucky. Did I feel lucky? Luck has had nothing to do with my miraculous recovery, to my mind. What has healed me—and continues to heal me—is a team effort of worldwide love and support, and a determination to use a combination of western medical approach with more integrative therapies. Plus, I look at this as an opportunity to deeply heal at a soul level through energy medicine and made the conscious choice to approach *everything* in my healing journey from a place of curious fascination. In my exploration of quantum healing, I have heard it said that brain tumours are "energetic brain injuries" and thus, may be healed using energy medicine modalities. That has certainly been my experience! I have dubbed this my "Healing Journey Back to My Soul" and have been documenting much of it quite publicly on social media. I have *never* once looked at this as anything but a blessing and a gift.

With the gift of this diagnosis, I had a great deal of healing work to do and was keen to immediately commence. One of the first traits I needed to acknowledge was that I am a perfectionist by nature, borne from an early childhood wound of believing I needed to prove myself worthy of love. I grew up a peacekeeper and people-pleaser as the second-born of four girls in my family. Also a high achiever, I believed I could do it all, with a smile, and was loath to say "no" to anyone asking for help with anything. I was Superwoman incarnate!

We had received the news in mid-December that our beloved dog, Scooby, had lymphoma. I was devastated and determined to do whatever I could to save him, despite his prognosis of one to four months tops. We had also received the news that my beautiful, gentle grandmother was likely not going to make it much past the holidays. But she had just turned 103 in early December and struggled with Alzheimer's, so her passing truly was a blessing. I had gotten to say my goodbye to her in July when I was visiting my family in New Brunswick. However, despite being able to rationalize her impending death, I found that I was turning inwards, getting quieter and quieter as I sank into sadness. I was struggling to put my thoughts into words, so was choosing not to speak at all, despite the never-ending thoughts buzzing through my brain.

In addition, I had noticed the week after Christmas that my hands were starting to shake, while my husband and I tried to make the best of the brutal cold at "SoLaCe", our cabin on Reid Lake. I had taken my sketchbook and other art supplies to do daily sketches and was noticing a tremor developing. I ignored it for the most part and was able to shrug it off to my anxiety and growing depression as well.

On New Year's Eve, I asked my husband to make a list of things we were grateful for in 2018. We were into Christmas number five without my cherished stepson, Luke, who adored the cabin in the short two years we had it while he was still alive. The "L" and the "C" in the name "SoLaCe" are capitalized in honour of his initials. At times, being at the cabin can be a melancholy-inducing experience, as we are often revisiting memories of Lukey. As we were wrapping up another year without him being physically with us, we were both grieving. Simultaneously, I was doing my best to count our blessings, knowing how possessing an attitude of gratitude is an essential practice for deep healing.

I also live in Yellowknife, Northwest Territories in Canada's North, and the winters are interminably long - especially the winter of the diagnosis, it seemed: brutally cold, and very dark. To have to go outside at all can feel like an insurmountable chore, but a necessity when one is a dog owner and holds down a job that requires one to leave the comfort of one's bed. By late November into December, I was counting down the days to Christmas Break.

What brought me north was a job; what keeps me here is my passion for the land, the proximity to countless clear and clean lakes, some of which get warm enough to swim in; and the fact that twenty years ago I fell in love with a man with a ready-made family. I am a high school art specialist who also teaches yoga, a course called Career and Life Management (aka CALM), and various other courses over the years. Sounds like an ideal job, doesn't it? It was pretty sweet most days, I will admit. I *loved* my work with students but recognized that the minutiae of the responsibilities of a teacher were increasing with each year.

As an internationally certified yoga instructor, I attempted to deal with my exhaustion by spending more time meditating, and specifically, exploring the technique of Yoga Nidra, which is well-documented to show how incredibly healing it is and far more beneficial than taking a nap. But I was burning out and recognized the desperate need for a break from teaching over the upcoming Christmas holidays. At that point, my manual dexterity had also started to suffer, and I was unable to type without errors—a lot of them. Also, I'd begun to notice my physical balance had started to suffer in early January. I would attempt to come into a pose that required moderate balance, such as Bird Dog (kneeling in a tabletop position with one arm and the opposite leg extended) and either fall over or come close to it.

3

As a natural communicator, I was beginning to have difficulty finding words. It wasn't a matter of not wanting to speak, but of not being able to put my thoughts into words. That worsened so much that my husband—not much of a talker to begin with—complained, "Why don't you talk to me anymore?" In our twenty years together, we had always been comfortable in silence and could go an hour or more without exchanging a word quite companionably. I struggled to respond, rarely doing much better than choking out, "I don't know what's going on. I don't know what's happening to me." We were both uncomfortable and confused by my developing difficulties and the inordinate amount of silence.

My grandmother passed on January 8th and I was numb, feeling nothing at all; at least for much of that night after receiving the call from my father. I could barely speak at all and I didn't cry initially. I even went to work the day after my grandmother's death. That day, however, I had a complete emotional breakdown in front of my first period Art 10 class. I couldn't stop sobbing. I went downhill from there, excusing myself from my yoga class to go out into the hallway to sob. I took the next three days off as compassionate leave.

On Friday, January 11th, I'd booked an acupuncture appointment to help balance me. Though it was very challenging walking there: I had no energy. Once I arrived, it was like a counselling session for the first third of the session. I actually felt a lot better after and decided to treat myself to an Epsom salts bath at home upon my return. I was home alone with the dogs as my husband was at work. I got the water ready and gratefully climbed into the tub. It was here that I soon lost track of time. At one point, I experienced what can only be described as the most surreal episode of my life to date. Suddenly I felt an indescribable rush of energy coming up through my feet, into my legs, trunk, my arms, out my fingers, and then up into my head. It literally felt like my head was exploding from both the front and the back so that I had to grasp onto the side of the tub. Once the initial waves subsided, I had the wherewithal to drain the tub. I sat, still conscious but stunned, upright in the tub, head pounding, wondering what on God's green Earth had just happened to me.

I had no sense of time throughout this episode. Once the water drained, I became chilled. I attempted, and failed, to get myself out of the tub. I had no strength, particularly on the right side of my body. Eventually, I was able through sheer strength of will, to lift myself up to sit on the edge of the tub; then on the toilet seat; then eased my way to a wobbly standing position. I have no recollection how long I stood but was able to weakly towel myself off and get my housecoat on, though the motor control was an issue.

When my husband got home from work, I tried to describe my experience. Being a problem-solver, his ready solution was to say, "There's extra-strength Advil in the cupboard; just take one or two and go to bed." I tease him about that response now, and he takes the ribbing. Neither of us suspected the seriousness and severity of what was happening to me. Taking the Advil did nothing to take away the pain in my head, nor could I sleep. It didn't occur to either of us to go to the hospital that night. As the weekend progressed, I deteriorated further, experiencing episodes of vertigo and headaches, but had made a commitment to teach a sold-out monthly offering of "Restorative Yoga and Healing Gong" session that I'd been offering on that Sunday night. That involved going by the high school where I teach to pick up extra props to ensure every participant had all that they required. It was hellish to make multiple trips up and down the stairs, not only at the school, but upon arrival at the yoga space, as it's on the building's lower level. Luckily, I was able to take the elevator one floor down. Looking back, I truly have no idea how I made it through those hours of hauling equipment, setting up, struggling to communicate, and guiding participants in and out of poses. In the last twenty minutes of the practice, as I was setting up to play the gong, I discovered that I wasn't even able to hold onto the three-pound mallet with my right hand; so I played with my non-dominant left hand.

When I got home, I asked my husband to take me to the Primary Care Centre the next morning, recognizing I needed to be looked at, but still not admitting that it might be serious enough to go to the Emergency Department instead. It is difficult to explain, and perhaps in hindsight, it is the way I was raised to brush things off, but I was convinced what I had experienced wasn't worthy of a trip to Emergency. Having to drive all the way to the other side of town to the hospital seemed to be too much of a hassle that bitterly cold morning.

On Monday morning, my husband dropped me off downtown at the Primary Care Centre on his way to work. I was entirely spaced out and growing quite distraught at the amount of time I had to wait to see a doctor. Eventually, I did get in and had a great deal of difficulty describing my symptoms. The kind, young doctor said, "Let's rule out the worst case scenario right away and get you a requisition for a CT scan." In *my* mind, however, I was thinking, *What? What do you mean worst case scenario? There's nothing wrong with my brain!* I left and haltingly walked the relatively short distance home. It was two weeks before I heard from Primary Care with a date for my CT scan. It was going to be a full four weeks—February 24th, before I was booked in. If I had taken my symptoms more seriously then, I would've been more assertive in ensuring I was seen in a timelier manner.

I was still on compassionate leave and in regular contact with my admin at the high school. I had found a sub to teach my Monday lunch hour "Mindful Movement and Meditation" class for the rest of the month, which was truly a blessing. I was still teaching my regular Wednesday "Kundalini Yoga for Stress Relief" class though—with difficulty, mind you. Another thing I didn't relinquish was to offer a four-week "Art and Yoga of Mandala" preregistered series in the month of January. Despite feeling a sense of dread about it through the latter half of December, it was sold-out. I forced myself to teach those five, two-hour classes on Monday evenings. It became quite apparent to my participants that I was struggling as the weekly sessions progressed. I did my best to put up a good front, and readily accepted potential explanations like, "It may be an inner ear infection," as my mother-in-law had suggested. Given how my husband had described my symptoms to her, that is valid. One of my fellow souls at Collective Soul Space had mentioned to me when I asked her to sub one of my classes, "Mo, there's far more to this than an inner ear infection; you really need to get this checked out!" Of note, I was told when I went to Primary Care that my ears were clear and that it definitely was not an inner ear infection.

My husband had two annual boys' trips pre-planned in the month of January, and though he was becoming growingly concerned as to my wellbeing, he left for Palm Springs to golf with buddies that he'd known for fifty years. I certainly wasn't going to begrudge him that. Besides, I still had art portfolios to grade and report cards to muddle through, so I had a great deal to keep me occupied. What should have been my normal five-hour process of entering grades and comments turned out to be a hellish marathon of entering, re-entering, and retyping due to repeated typos. Having experienced the trauma of my grade six math teacher telling me in front of the class that I was stupid, I was reminded of the importance of taking care with one's words when communicating with students. I didn't always get it right, particularly in my early days and in the heat of the moment, but providing personalized comments was important to me. As a result, it was a hellishly frustrating and exhausting period of at least three days to get the report cards done.

By mid-week, I was emotionally spent, and had additional episodes of vertigo and was experiencing increasing numbers of crying jags. I drove myself to the Emergency Department as I was home alone. I truly should not have been behind the wheel. I saw the same doctor that I had seen at Primary Care. I could barely get any words out between tears, but I told him that I thought that part of my issue was the grief of my dog's terminal illness, and that perhaps my grandmother's recent death triggered residual grief over my twenty-one-year-old stepson's tragic death. He said to me, "Maureen, I'm going to stop you right there and give you a prescription for an Emergency Mental Health Clinic appointment." He came back a few minutes later and handed me a paper that had a phone number and a scheduled time. I was to take myself to the Mental Health Clinic, located in the same building as Primary Care, the next day. I did. In the two days that followed, I had completed a questionnaire, with much difficulty as my manual dexterity was faulty at best and even had an appointment with a psychiatrist. At this appointment, I received a prescription for drugs to help me sleep, a diagnosis of severe depression and anxiety, and another prescription for the anxiety. I was also given a sick leave note from the psychiatrist to pass on to my admin and the board office. None of this felt right to me, but I was still unwilling to consider that what I was experiencing was neurological. After all, I have always been so healthy. Besides, depression runs on both sides of my family, so it wasn't implausible.

I phoned my husband the night I got back, crying, saying that I was overwhelmed and needed to cut back on my workload. His kind response was, "Maureen, your mental health is what's most important. Whatever we need to do, we'll make it work. Go part-time if you need to; don't worry about the money."

Meanwhile, my days were filled with naps on our sectional sofa with at least one of the dogs and watching health and quantum science videos on the subscription website, Gaia. In particular, I was becoming increasingly enthralled with the series by Gregg Braden called "Missing Links". With each episode a highly digestible half-hour, I would watch several back-to-back. I couldn't get enough of the episodes relating to Heart-Brain Coherence and the revelations of the relatively new science of Quantum Energy.

In the darkening days of autumn, I had also developed a daily practice of listening to and practicing various meditations on the Insight Timer App. There, I was introduced to Sarah Blondin who deeply resonated with her "Live Awake" podcast sessions. I then purchased the premium version of Insight Timer so that I could access their ten-day courses. I completed a number of them such as: "Coming Home to Yourself" by Sarah Blondin, "Knowing Your

Soul's True Purpose" by Kim Newing, Self-Care Healing Spaces for Grief and Loss" by Judith Campbell, and "Your Guide to Deeper Sleep" by Jennifer Piercey. My subscription continues to be worth every penny.

I also discovered Irene Lyon on YouTube. Based out of North Vancouver, she is a trauma and nervous system dysregulation specialist, skilled in aiding viewers to learn how to strengthen, heal, and bring the nervous system into regulation through somatic modalities. I have always been fascinated with learning, and though I pursued fine arts in university, in more recent years, the science of energy—quantum science—as well as biology and chemistry as they pertain in particular to our ability to heal ourselves, have become a preoccupation.

Robert returned from Palm Springs long enough to do laundry and check in with me. I was going to my bi-weekly appointments with my mental health case worker and she and I would talk about my past and what might have triggered my anxiety and depression. I still struggled to find my words, so communication remained painfully challenging.

Though really uncomfortable leaving me alone, my husband left a few days later to fly to Montreal to catch some Habs hockey with his buddies. He was reassured, however, that my best friend, Natalie, was coming up from Calgary to keep me company while he was away. She arrived later on the same day that he'd departed. Nat was *so* nurturing and kind, and with lots of experience interacting with people with anxiety and depression, she did her best to problem-solve and help to make me well again. We got outside every day to walk the dogs, and though at this point, I was starting to struggle to lift my right foot, it was only obvious to me. The weather remained dreadfully cold, and while I recognized that though exercise and fresh air are normally great antidotes to anxiety and depression, all they did was add to my exhaustion.

February 3, 2019 Photo credit: Natalie Sweet

Nat did all of the cooking, cleaning, and grocery shopping, which included shopping for adult diapers for me as I had no bladder control at this point...now *that* is a bestie! She communicated her concern for my well-being not only to me but she was also in close contact with my identical twin sister, Kirsten. It was during my time with Nat that we agreed that a change of scenery was perhaps what I needed for what I was now referring to as my "Spiritual Crisis". Thus, I booked a ticket to spend some time with my twin sister in Abbotsford, B.C. for ten days, two days after Robert's return from Montreal.

Chapter 2

Spiritual Crisis

AS MY DEPRESSION deepened in January, I reached out for help to my friend and former yoga student, Jillian MacKay, a gifted yet humble healer who is trained in accessing the Akashic Records and various shamanic approaches. In a nutshell, the Akashic Records are a record of one's soul's journey through all planes and dimensions of consciousness, known or unknown. Although raised in a church-going family, at some point in my adulthood, I explored spirituality rather than traditional religion. I believe there is a higher power and I do believe in God, but I do not restrict my beliefs to Christianity. I do not feel the need for church in order to be faithful in my spirituality. With my spiritual beliefs, it made sense to reach out to someone trained in accessing other realms. I had done so with someone else trained in Soul Journeys™ certification after my stepson Luke died and I found great healing in knowing that he was still with us as a guide—our "Spirit Bear".

I first reached out to Jillian on January 27th, 2019 with the following plea: "What are you up to between Feb 5 and 8? I am on leave from work and am hoping you can help. It is a Spiritual Crisis and I need to get away. I have SO much anger that it is impacting my entire life. I hope you are able to house me...and heal me. I'd be happy to pay you." I truly appreciated her same-day response and discipline in setting boundaries. "Take a deep breath...dear one. You are loved beyond measure. I would be happy to have a session with you, and you do not have to be in my home to have it. 100% of my business is over the phone. It is more powerful actually." She then directed me to her website, saying that she agreed that a change of atmosphere helps and that I would find my healing path.

Interestingly, within two days of that message exchange, Jill reached out to me on with the following message:

"Maureen,

I've been debating whether or not to send you this... so here goes:

I feel your desperation to resolve this. I feel the rage within you. Yet...I cannot "heal" you...you have to "allow" the healing. It's a 50/50 deal...I download and transmit, and you allow the receiving energetically. I know your brain will say "I want healing" yet your energetic field is communicating something different.

We will definitely go into your Akash and see what is going on...that is guaranteed. This I feel is very deeply buried...and that's why I offered the package to you...as you'll need time to "allow" the giving up of this.

To prepare you for our session...feel into the phrase "What is the payback to me for keeping this rage?"

I don't need an answer...I just want you to start FEELING where it hits you in your body...how it makes you feel...etc."

I let her know how much I appreciated her response and to remind me how much I was loved and could let go of what doesn't serve me. Easier said than done, this letting go process! I informed her before our first session that I would continue to book session after session as long as it took me for the healing to be received. I received one more communication from her prior to our first session. It was a link to "Light Languages and Harmonic Healing for Wounds of the Heart" and I was advised to listen to it in a relaxed state and to consume water to ground myself after. I did, and it was a really strange and new experience! Light Languages is a modality that uses sound vibration through the practitioners' vocal chords but doesn't use a recognizable language. I felt remarkably better that morning than in the previous couple of days.

It was February 5th when we had our first phone session from the comfort of my home yoga and meditation space. It was supposed to have been a ninety-minute session; however, I had such a strong emotional response within the first hour that I "shut down" and we terminated the session early. What brought on such a strong response? After she gained my permission to access my Akashic Records—having the subject's permission is absolutely required—my guides (the Record Keepers) asked me if I had ever been sexually assaulted as a child? I froze, thinking, "I haven't told a SOUL about what happened to me, not even my twin sister!" I started to cry and was able to haltingly explain that in fact, yes, I had been molested by my adopted cousin in my parents' home when we were both seven. It was important for me to note that it was not a blood relative, so for some reason, that made a difference to me. For forty-seven years, I had not told anyone because I was ashamed! I have carried that shame with me for decades, and it's impacted my personality and some of my actions to be sure. Repressing one's trauma results in the creation of stories that literally become part of our genetic makeup.

Jillian asked me to feel into the rage and let my cousin know just how it affected me. I wasn't able to. My tears flowed faster, my throat closed off, and I could feel my bladder needing to void (or wanting to empty). Out of the norm, Jillian attempted to prompt me into expressing my rage by letting me know what she was "hearing", using shockingly strong language that definitely echoed what I had been tamping down. But I still couldn't express myself and rushed to the toilet. Upon my return, she acknowledged that our work was done for now, as I'd gone into "shut down". She offered to take the thirty minutes remaining in our session and add it to the next one, which I greatly appreciated. For the rest of the day I did my best to rest but wet myself three times between my mindfulness meditation sessions and a throat chakra healing and a fourth time while soaking in the bathtub. I was a mess.

Jillian followed up with me that evening, assuring me that I was on the road to recovery by allowing the feelings to surface, to feel them, then release them. The next day, she reached out to let me know she'd been guided to send me "The Forgiveness Decree", which was channelled to her by the Record Keepers within the Akashic Records. It is a very powerful spoken prayer and she invited me to treat it as a forty-day practice to start moving the energy in my body: to feel and release the blocks through emotional release. Apparently, she'd felt an emotional release when I cried during our session the previous morning. I took her advice and started reciting the prayer at least once a day; once I began, it didn't take long for me to experience the benefits of this practice. I've included it here because once I started telling my friends and some family members about this practice in the spring, they wanted me to send them a copy.

The Forgiveness Decree

I forgive everyone who has ever hurt or harmed me,
consciously or unconsciously, in this life or any other.
In every plane, level or dimension known or unknown.
I offer them Grace.

I ask for forgiveness for anyone I have ever hurt or
harmed, consciously or unconsciously, in this life or
any other.
In every plane, level or dimension known or unknown.
I ask for Grace.

I forgive myself for anything I have ever done to hurt or
harm myself or another, consciously or unconsciously,
in this life or any other, in this universe or any other.
In every plane, level or dimension known or unknown.
I accept Grace.

Powerful words, aren't they? I started strong but didn't integrate the decree daily right away. Once I did, I certainly began to experience the benefits of this forgiveness practice.

Prior to our next session, I was flying to Abbotsford for a change of atmosphere; to get away from the dark, the excessive cold, and the snow. I had booked my ticket for the afternoon of February 10th and I was due to arrive in Abbotsford by 10:00 pm. When my husband reluctantly dropped me off at the Yellowknife airport, I was still in survival mode but I also intuitively recognized that I was making a mistake by travelling. The Universe agreed with me! There was a highly unusual snowstorm happening in the Fraser Valley, and I sat in the Edmonton airport for several hours before being able to board my connecting flight to Abbotsford. Over those hours, I was deteriorating physically, so that by the time we boarded and landed in Abbotsford, I wasn't able to lift my right arm or make any real use of it: plus I was really dragging my right foot as I wasn't able to lift it. It was 2:00 am and I felt like I could collapse at any moment.

Kirsten was shocked when she saw me struggle to walk towards her at the airport. We kissed and hugged one another tightly for a long time. I apologized as best as I could given my difficulties communicating for not being entirely up front with her about my condition. Distraught, but putting on a brave face, Kirsten served as a prop for me to walk toward the baggage carousel, carried my bag for me, and helped me to her vehicle. We drove through the dying storm to her townhouse where she carried my bag upstairs while I gingerly pulled myself up the stairs. We were both exhausted, so agreed to chat more after a good night's sleep. We embraced and kissed once more, and I crawled into bed and slept deeply.

Knowing how much I enjoyed "floating"—that is, soaking in sensory deprivation tanks—Kirsten had booked me in for a session the next morning. Floating can be an incredibly powerful meditative experience! I had been introduced to the concept in Kitsilano, a neighbourhood in Vancouver, a few years prior and fell in love with the experience. I was healthier then, obviously. If I'd been of clear mind, I would have cancelled my upcoming appointment, but I still somehow believed that it might help me. Kirsten set me up with a hiking pole to help me to walk more easily. She dropped me off at the newly opened

Float House in Abbotsford after we agreed to meet up for lunch a couple of stores down at a predetermined time.

The session was almost torturous. It was a challenge to get undressed by myself and a massive struggle to get myself in the cabin/tank. Once in, I was able to relax, at least until I realized my bladder was about to empty. I fought in the darkened cabin to orient myself to open the heavy door. I barely got the provided housecoat on and to the bathroom in time. But I didn't make it to the toilet. I was humiliated as I mopped the bathroom floor with an available facecloth. I shamefacedly made my way back to my room where I crawled gingerly back into the tank for my remaining time. When my time was up, I bruised myself as I struggled to extract myself from the tank, shower, dry off, and get dressed to meet Kirsten.

Zuzu and I lying on sofa in Richmond

After lunch, we made our way to Richmond, where we were going to be house-sitting and pet-sitting there for the remainder of my stay for long-time friends of Kirsten's. We were looking forward to it. It was a bungalow, so no significant stairs for me and they had a hot tub. Plus, their wee dog Zuzu turned out to be sweet and affectionate, their cat being much choosier. Kirsten became my primary caretaker, making all meals, cleaning up, and attempting to get me outside for her daily walks with Zuzu. I spent most of the time on the loveseat, napping, and listening to Insight Timer meditations and talks. Zuzu got into the habit of lying on me. We figured she definitely picked up that I was sick, as she would oftentimes lie near my head.

Answers of a Sort

Jillian's and my next session was life-changing in the sense that I got an energetic answer as to what was going on with me. As I was lying on the loveseat in the living room wearing headphones for my session; Kirsten was in the bedroom with the door closed so as not to disturb me. We began our Channelling session, which is slightly different from the Harmonic Frequencies/Light Languages session as it focuses on allowing spirit guides, light beings, and angels to come through even more readily. I still get teary when I think about that session. In fact, my throat is closing, and I am feeling the tears now as I type this, because my stepson came through loud and clear. His repeated message to me—truly, each time he's come through since he left his physical body—is that he was brought into my life to teach me what it meant to be unconditionally loved. I'd always struggled with accepting that—not just by him, but unconditionally loved *by anyone*; but at this point, I was more receptive to this message now: that he would always be in my life and that to please know just how much he loved me. That was as much of the session as I shared with Kirsten. I elected to keep the rest from her because it went pretty "woo-woo", as I like to say, and I wasn't sure that she would be open to hearing what was communicated to me.

What follows may be challenging for many to accept or believe. Prior to my work with Jillian, I did not have much, if any experience with communicating with Light Beings, but somehow when the Pleiadeans came through I had a complete and utter sense of trust and belief in what was being shared. What fascinates me still is that I had no fear then, nor have I since receiving their messages.

In a strange tone of voice (almost like a sensation without being a sound) and yet a foreign-sounding but indistinguishable accent, I was informed by the Pleiadeans as channelled by Jillian that:

> "We're sorry that it's come to this, but you've not been listening to nor making use of the unique gifts that you've been given in this life. So, we've put something in your brain SO deep that it will defy logic. It will be considered incurable, but you **will** be able to heal yourself **if** you tap into and make use of your gifts."

An eerie calm came over me and I knew then that I'd be all right. Truly. I just knew somehow to the depth of my being that I would be fine. I don't recall much of the rest of the call, except that I knew I had to say a quick goodbye to Jillian once we'd closed my Akashic Records for the session in order for me to make it to the toilet!

We booked our next Harmonic Frequencies/Light Languages session for the following week. That session never happened, as that morning after an emergency CT scan of my head, I was medivaced to Edmonton.

In the months following, there have been several communications with the Pleiadeans and other Light Beings, many archangels, angels, and goddesses. Incredibly, during a session in April, Jillian informed me: "I have Jesus of Nazareth here with me and he would like to lay healing hands on your head." I was bathed in a golden, healing light around my head—I could feel the energy!

Without question, I consider the work I have done with Jillian and the Record Keepers—my guides, to be instrumental in my continued healing. We have been peeling away the layers over time to heal energetic injuries and trauma that have taken place over lifetimes. I honestly do not think I'd be where I am today without our work together. Though we had two sessions per month in the early stages of my healing journey, it currently feels more like we are on a maintenance schedule of once every four to six weeks and depends on when I feel like I need a tune-up or tweaking.

Chapter 3

No Room for Denial

Feeling Helpless

BEFORE EITHER OF us realized just how sick I was, Kirsten had bought me a ticket to join her and another friend to see Justin Timberlake at the Rogers Arena in Vancouver on February 15th for his *Man of the Woods* Tour. At that point, I *really* did not want to go, but was not about to cancel as Kirsten didn't feel comfortable leaving me by myself; plus, it would have been a waste of her generous gift. We had agreed to meet a friend of hers who I knew as an acquaintance for dinner in Chinatown before the show. I laboriously walked there from our parking spot at Rogers Arena. I was using a gigantic umbrella as a walking stick, though it was a bit drizzly. I linked arm-in-arm with Kirsten while she put the umbrella up. The walk felt interminable. I found the restaurant excessively loud and found myself near or in tears for much of the time. I have no recollection of what I ate, only that it was supremely difficult for me to feed myself. I almost fell down the stairs en route to the bathroom and having to exert a great deal of effort to make it back up the stairs. The walk back to Rogers Arena felt even longer and slower than the walk to the restaurant and I still had to somehow get through the JT concert.

The man is a brilliant performer and his entourage is amazingly talented as well. However, I was overwhelmed and preoccupied with figuring out how to not wet myself too many times in the adult diaper that I was now sporting 24/7. That was an abject failure. More than once, I had to struggle up the stairs in the arena, making my way to the ladies' room and grapple with changing said diaper for another using only one hand. I was once more feeling entirely humiliated by my state.

The concert could not end soon enough for me. We left just before the encore, beating the crowds and slowly making our way to Kirsten's car to drive back to Richmond.

A few days into my visit, she had started to encourage me to go see a neurologist or neurosurgeon upon my return to Yellowknife. She had also suggested that we consider going to the hospital in Richmond. We come from stubborn stock and I was very resistant to going to a hospital in a city I'm not familiar with. At that point, there was absolutely NO denying that my symptoms were neurological, but I figured I could wait until I was home before seeing a doctor. My physical balance and sense of orientation had started to deteriorate further and by the second half of my ten-day visit, I had started falling over. The first two times happened in the bedroom where Kirsten and I were sharing a king-sized bed. The first time, I fell into the bed when trying to make the bed. I was on the side by the mirrored closet doors. The second time I fell over, I actually fell into the mirrored doors, and was shocked that I didn't shatter the mirrors. I did knock everything but the lamp off the nightstand, which was embarrassing. It terrified Kirsten. She came rushing into the bedroom to check on me as I was rather precariously attempting to upright myself.

It was my third fall that was the most dangerous. That night, we had decided to go into the hot tub with Kirsten preceding me, ensuring the lights were on in the tub. The exterior lights were not on, though. It was dark as pitch. I completely lost my orientation when I took a step forward and missed the step, falling in a heap onto the cold, icy deck. Very fortunately avoiding cracking my head on the side of the tub, I lost it then, sobbing as though my heart was breaking. Stunned, Kirsten leapt out of the tub and rushed to me. Gathering me in her arms, holding and rocking me gently, she asked if I was all right. Physically I was all right, aside from what became a colourful reminder of my fall—a vivid purple bruise on my right hip and butt cheek. Emotionally and physically, I remained very tender for the remaining days of my visit.

Despite my progressing difficulties, we filled our time together with much laughter, dancing (as best I could), singing, and getting outdoors. In fact, we would sometimes burst into spontaneous tear-provoking laughter that were anyone to witness, they would have been perplexed as to the reason. Our twin humour was as strong as ever. Kirst was helping me dress, and like a mother with a young child, assisted me putting on my boots and jacket. Her care and concern meant everything to me. One night, we hunkered down to watch the documentary *HEAL* on Netflix. It was the first of several times watching it over the next couple of months. We also showed it to our parents in March. This time we watched it with me lying down on the loveseat wrapped in a couple of blankets, and Kirsten on the floor beside me. Part of what I loved about this documentary is that it echoed everything I believed about the body's ability to heal itself through the use of energy medicine, the importance of self-education, mindset, and the practice of gratitude. Another day, close to the end of my stay, we ventured to Steveston: a beautifully scenic riverside town, where we slowly walked the boardwalk, stopping often, and having a delicious lunch at one of the many seafood restaurants. What should have been a delightful experience of pampering, getting a pedicure was excessively overstimulating with the noise of the television and the genuinely concerned questioning from the esthetician: "What happened to you?" and "Are you going to be okay?"

I found out later from Kirst how guilty she felt for not taking me to the hospital and how she felt she should have done more. I never once held her at fault. They were my decisions to make: ones which I chose to avoid making. I do not hold myself to blame either, as I don't believe that it serves any purpose. In my heart of hearts, I still maintain that everything transpired as it needed to. I needed to get as sick as I did in order to grasp the gravity of my deterioration and required healing.

My trip home to Yellowknife dawned clear and it was still dark when we hit the road early to drive from Richmond to Abbotsford airport. We sat in the café for a while and Kirsten had breakfast and I had tea, as I wasn't hungry. I was in such a blurry state of mind that I almost forgot to hug her goodbye as I made my way towards security! We had a good chuckle over that. I did my best to get comfortable in the large waiting area, but I was getting progressively mentally foggier and all tasks were tiring. Now hungry and not knowing just how long we'd be waiting, I undertook with some difficulty peeling a grapefruit that I'd brought with me and noshed on some nuts and seeds. It was a challenge to contain my temper as the flight was further delayed with no explanation forthcoming.

Two hours after our original scheduled departure, we loaded onto the plane. I sat in the correct row but wrong seat, so moved when a young mom with her baby showed up to sit in the seat I had been mistakenly occupying. I looked up and saw the RCMP walking towards us. The reason they were on the plane became clear within seconds. They were on the plane to escort the young mom and baby off the plane! I was devastated for her, as I'd been picking up on some intuitive "hits" that she was likely fleeing a hostile living environment. I have no proof of this; it's just what I suspected based on her body language. With a defeated air, she and her adorable but anxious baby went along with the RCMP.

I was totally discombobulated when I arrived in Edmonton. I was unaware of my connecting gate but made my way to the bathroom upstairs, soaking my diaper on the way. Good thing I'd learned to pack diapers with me! I was beyond humiliation at this point. As it turned out I didn't need to have climbed the stairs, as my gate was back where I'd started: perhaps two away! I was unbelievably frustrated with myself. I took my time getting back down the stairs, doing my best to avoid making eye contact with anyone, though I could certainly feel their eyes on me. I'm certain I appeared inebriated to other passengers. Given the length of time I've lived in the north, it's rare that I don't see at least a few familiar faces on flights from Edmonton to Yellowknife. I saw a former student of mine, en route to one of the diamond mine sites, but I avoided making eye contact with her and she either didn't recognize me or pretended not to, which I was fine with.

Kirsten had paid the extra fee for me to fly Plus, though it really doesn't make a difference in the small Q400s that fly to Yellowknife. I did appreciate the gesture, as she'd done so as to put me in the first row right across from the wee bathroom stall at the front of the plane. I dozed a bit, but was mostly in anxious agony, desperate to get home. Since the unfortunate decision to downsize airplanes was made the year before, the previously one-and-a-half-hour flight was now two hours long but it felt like five to my beleaguered brain. I was self-conscious of my appearance, seeing the strange looks I'd been getting from fellow passengers. Did it appear that I was under the influence of drugs or alcohol?

I was the first to disembark. I was very slow moving to the terminal, therefore not the first person in the building. Robert met me and I learned later that based on my appearance, he was convinced I'd had a stroke. Right after he hugged and kissed me, his first words to me were, "I'm taking you to Emergency in the morning." I didn't disagree. He carried my bag to the truck and had to help me with my seatbelt. It was a quiet ride home. I picked up on his fear and an underlying frustration at not being aware of my deterioration. Just like I hadn't been entirely open with Kirsten as to my condition prior to my trip to B.C, nor had I been honest with the level of my decline whenever Robert and I talked on the phone while I was away. We slept fitfully, and when his alarm went off at 6:45 am, he hopped in the shower. I fell back to sleep until he flicked on the overhead light and using a voice that brooked no room for argument, told me to get up and get dressed as he was taking me to the Emergency department. I did so with difficulty, crying after he went out to start his truck, leaving me alone to struggle with my boots. I went outside with only one arm through my coat as I was unable to get my coat on. Once more, he had to help me to fasten my seatbelt, and we drove to the hospital.

Trust Me!

When asked to describe what brought me in, I told the triage nurse that I believed that perhaps I'd had a TIA: a mini-stroke. There is a family history of them, in fact, I had a younger sister who survived a massive stroke at the age of thirty-eight. My blood pressure was taken, and I was admitted. My husband joined me and while we waited for a doctor to see us, there was another nurse who came in. Recognizing my name, she mentioned that her mother was a yoga student in my classes and spoke very highly of me. She was incredibly sweet, kind, and very efficient. The doctor on call came in and got a sense of what had been going on with me. She had me go for an immediate CT scan, which I'd been somewhat familiar with for other body parts, just never my head! There was no real sense of time after that. After I was wheeled back to my cubicle, the attending doctor came in to deliver the news to my husband and myself. There was evidence of lesions on the brain and I was to be medivaced to the University of Alberta Hospital (UAH) in Edmonton as soon as a plane could be made available.

As mentioned, I had experienced no fear since receiving the news from the Pleiadeans that there was something placed in my brain that would defy logic. However, seeing as I hadn't communicated that nugget to anyone, my husband was not without fear; in fact, he was terrified and devastated, but is also very good at dealing with emergencies. He called my parents and did his best to communicate the news when he didn't even know what "lesions on the brain" necessarily meant; thus trying to explain it to Mom and Dad was a challenge. Meanwhile, the kind nurse came back in to set me up with an IV of what turned out to be a megadose of dexamethasone: a drug used to reduce inflammation in the brain. It is frequently prescribed for people with brain tumours and I was certainly glad for it for the time I was on it, as it allowed me to function somewhat normally within a relatively short period of time. I got a chance to speak with my parents, naively telling them not to worry, that I'd be fine! I believed it with my whole heart, but convincing my husband and family was going to be a challenge. My parents were left with the responsibility to call each of my sisters and extended family members with the shocking news.

I'd received a message from Jillian asking me if I'd like to rebook our session that had been scheduled for 11:00 am; it was 11:06 at that point. I responded: "Thanks Jill! I'm being medivaced. I will let you know." Her response was to, "Please take care." Meanwhile, Robert had ample time while we waited for the medevac to go home, pack a bag for each of us, and make his way back as we'd learned that he'd be allowed to accompany me down to Edmonton on the medevac. In shock and in tears, he held my hand saying, "I can't lose another person that I love." I told him that I wasn't going anywhere. He had to have faith, to trust me. This was all part of the Universe's Great Plan for me. He just had to trust. Easy for me to say! What became a bit of a recording on my part, I told him, "This is just a chapter in *The Book of Mo*, and it's certainly not the final chapter!" Another emergency nurse who is a long-time friend came by in tears to say goodbye and that she knew I'd be all right. She leaned over me in the bed that was being wheeled toward the waiting ambulance, kissing my forehead.

Feeling no pain and still no fear, we loaded into the ambulance and made our way to the hangar.

Chapter 4

Lessons in Compassion

I WAS TRANSFERRED TO an ambulance to get to UAH. Fortunately, the ambulance driver didn't have the siren on, which would definitely have made the ride untenable given my sensitivity to sound. Paperwork necessitated my waiting in the hallway. The noise bothered me a great deal. At my request, Robert asked if I could be moved to a quieter spot while waiting for a curtained cubicle. I kept getting asked repeatedly if I was in any pain, which I wasn't. My condition created a feeling like the wait was never-ending. The one highlight, if I could use that term, was to see a former student, Shannon—now an Emergency Nurse, on my floor. She was stunned to see me in my current state but upon learning why I was medivaced down, she hugged me and said that she would check on me when she could, despite not being assigned to my area, and that I was to reach out to her if I needed anything.

Soon after our arrival to the cubicle, my twin sister arrived, entirely distraught and guilt-ridden for not having insisted on taking me to the hospital in Richmond. She'd received a phone call from our parents sharing that I had lesions on my brain. I was entirely grateful that she'd basically dropped everything in order to be by my side, though not at all surprised. I've gained a new level of respect and adoration for my beloved twinnie.

The hours that we waited in the noisy ER mounted and became sensorially painful in that my neighbour on the other side of the curtain was seemingly suffering from a mental illness relating to hypochondria. She was incredibly loud and insistent on repeatedly telling her story to whomever would listen We were given no option due to her volume. Given the audible conversations with the treaters, it became apparent that she was a bit of a regular at the ER. It was late when she was finally sent home. She'd been insisting on an MRI, convinced that she had MS. She was sent home while I was getting another CT scan. Sadly, there was still no sleep to be had, as with her gone, the cubicle was filled by a most unfortunate fellow who was in really rough shape in the sense that he had no bowel control. The stench was smothering, and the poor clean-up crew had to come at least three times to scour and sterilize the area using very loud motorized equipment. By this point, after trying to sleep on her jacket on the floor my twin sister had gone to a quiet seating area to attempt to get some sleep. My husband was on the floor to my left, understandably unable to sleep.

At 4:00 am I was "rescued" and moved to what's known as the Rapid Transfer Unit (RTU). It's the newest area in the hospital, and thanks to a peppy and personality-filled nurse who took me under her wing, I was given a corner unit with actual walls on all sides! There was a curtain instead of a door, but it sure as heck beat anywhere in either of the hospitals I had spent time in over the previous twenty-four hours! The purpose of the RTU is for patients to be in a more comfortable spot for a few hours to a day before they are transferred to the unit where they are going. In my case, that was Neurosurgery. Because I was such a "good patient", Sheila, the nurse who'd taken a shining to me, kept sending other patients upstairs to the overcrowded Neurosurgery unit while I relaxed in relative comfort. I was blissfully ignorant of her actions until what would have been my fourth night in the RTU, when she came to tell me that she was being forced to move me upstairs. I had started to feel quite at home in my relatively beautiful space with its new furnishings, but I completely understood.

In the time that I was in RTU, we met with the Neurosurgeon assigned to my case. My lawyer twin sister peppered him with questions. She had researched him and wasn't pleased with what she'd read about his no-nonsense, abrupt communication style or specific area of expertise. She didn't believe he was the right person to perform the biopsy or, if necessary, operate on her beloved twin's brain. Kirst was also very assertive in her insistence that I be seen as soon as possible for my MRI. To her mind, they were being too slow to get this essential test run; she had a valid point. However, because I appeared so calm and functional, they didn't consider my case an emergency, and there were at least five emergency MRI's that needed to be taken before mine.

It became a bit of a waiting game, with me lying blissfully chipper and pain-free in bed, while my husband and twinnie (as we'd begun to refer to one another) fretted and paced. Fortunately, I had a couple of visitors in RTU; my sister-in-law Laurie had been visiting one of her daughters and her family in Leduc (south of Edmonton), so was very anxious to see me when she heard the news. I was having a much easier time communicating now, as the dexamethasone pills I was taking every few hours were having a hugely beneficial effect. After hugs, kisses, tears, and "I love you", she, Robert, and Kirsten took a break from the hospital and went to Earls restaurant. While they were out, I made the conscious decision to go public on Facebook and posted a "Full Disclosure" with a photo of Kirsten and me snuggled in my hospital bed together in the RTU, explaining what I understood at that time. The outpouring of support was instantaneous. Hundreds of people responded with shock and dismay, but also with their love, prayers, and what I'd referred to as "good juju". I communicated that I was currently in a holding pattern as I was on a waitlist to have an MRI.

"Twin Power Unite!"

I began to receive text messages as well as—all expressing their support and love. A dear friend and former co-worker, Janina, came by my second night in RTU and gifted me a handmade mala bracelet that I have worn every day since receiving it. I heard from one of my identical twin stepsons that same night. We had a touching and hilarious exchange relating to how I'd always stressed to their father when they were growing up, the importance of recognizing him and his brother as individuals. I'd come into their lives when they were four and as an identical twin myself, recognized the absolute necessity to treat the boys as independent people. For reasons I understand but struggled with for a very long time (as it reinforced my self-limiting belief of worthiness), all of my husband's children except Luke were reticent to openly express their love for me until now. I consider my practice of The Forgiveness Decree to have played a part in the miracle of the boys now expressing that they did in fact love me.

That night I also received the offer of a huge gift from the manager of a fly-in eco lodge where I'd hosted yoga retreats. Katherine from Blachford Lake Lodge (BLL), 100 km northeast of Yellowknife, had consulted with the lodge owner and Mike, a long-time friend of my husband, and they offered us a complimentary trip for four (Robert, me, Mom, and Dad) to BLL once they reopened in June. I was blown away by the generous offer and let her know that we'd definitely take them up on it. The generous and unanticipated gifts kept coming as the days and weeks progressed.

Before being moved to the Neurosurgery Unit, I did manage to get my first MRI done on Sunday night. Being transported via wheelchair through the maze that is UAH into the bowels of the hospital where the concrete-lined walls house the MRI machine, I was really impressed by the art on the walls. I learned later that UAH has a highly valuable collection of artworks that they keep on permanent display. Fortunately, I do not suffer from claustrophobia, so the only thing that got to me was how loud the MRI machine was, despite the protective headphones I was sporting.

We waited for the MRI results as we'd been informed that it could take up to a week. Kirsten insisted to the neurosurgeon and his chief resident that was unacceptable given my state. She pressed to have the results released sooner. They agreed. I am so thankful for her assertiveness, as I know it was instrumental in achieving responsiveness in my favour.

"I could pee on this calendar!"

Misadventures in the Neurosurgery Unit

I was moved from the comfort of the RTU to the extreme discomfort of the cramped and overcrowded Neurosurgery Unit after my MRI. Without much in the way of communication, I was wheeled into a double room that had the curtain pulled across. I was informed that my roommate was a quadriplegic stroke survivor but that was it. I couldn't see him past the curtain. All I heard was the small television that was playing god-knows-what and the drone of a motorized bed that kept shifting angles every few minutes: I presumed to help prevent painful bedsores. I was aggravated by the noise to be sure, but too symptomatic to do anything about it. Earlier, Kirsten had gone to stay with a cousin about twenty minutes away and Robert in a hotel. The hours dragged on and I struggled to sleep due to the noise. Eventually, I got up to take a peek around the curtain and to my dismay, there was no one in the bed beside me! I was a bit peeved as I had believed he was sleeping, and I didn't want to wake him. I turned off the television and crawled back into my bed.

At one point close to midnight, I attempted to get up to go to the adjoining bathroom a few steps from my bed. I didn't make it to the toilet. I soaked my diaper, the floor, and my brand-new cozy socks that I'd received from my sister-in-law Laurie. I started sobbing so hard that the night charge nurse came in. Once she saw me in my state of emotional distress, she gathered me in her arms and hugged me so tightly. She spoke to me so softly as a mother would a child, while gently disrobing and re-dressing me, promising to wash the socks and return them to me. It was exactly what I needed at that moment.

My unfortunate roomie showed up at 1:00 am, being wheeled in by a couple of the night nurses. Considering his state—highly inebriated, hostile, crude, and unrepentant—I am still in admiration of the nurses' compassion towards him. If I thought it was a challenge to sleep before, I had no idea what I was in for. The nurses needed to re-insert his IV for his pain meds; however, his veins were collapsed from all his drug use. He was screaming epithets at the nurses and I was in the fetal position covering my ears to try and block him out. I have no recollection how long this went on, but not once did the nurses lose their patience with him. They managed to get his IV set up once more. I think they must have given him sedatives, or he just passed out, as once he got quiet, I believe I too passed out from exhaustion.

Both Kirsten and my husband arrived as soon as the hospital doors opened to the public. They peeked in on me, and seeing me dozing peacefully, went to a waiting room to wait for the Neurosurgery team to begin their rounds. We were hopeful to hear the results of the MRI that morning. Soon after, I was awakened by Kirst, who was a bit panicked to have returned to my room to find me sobbing as if my heart was breaking despite being asleep. The nurses were again by my roommate's bedside, and he was screaming in pain because they had to once again adjust his IV. My response to my sis was, "He's in such pain; he is in so much pain, I can't handle it!" I am an empath—naturally and intuitively attuned to the energy of others. It would appear that in my highly symptomatic state, my senses were in overdrive, even in my sleep!

Kirsten was somewhat relieved to hear why I had been so distraught, as she thought that perhaps she'd missed the Neurosurgery team doing their rounds. She had not. I briefed her on my experience in the early morning hours and she was not at all impressed and communicated this to the nurses to see if anything could be done. Soon after, one of the nurses on the morning shift came in with a massive bouquet of lilies, irises, and roses saying "Gee, I wish I was as loved as you are!" They were from my sister's law firm; I was blown away by the gesture.

Because of my numerous pre-existing dietary restrictions, the dietician came in that morning to discuss what hospital food I'd be able to consume, seeing as they were worried that I wasn't consuming enough calories. It was a bit of a disaster because I was insistent that "sugar feeds tumours" to which she defensively responded, "There's no evidence of that." I had to seriously bite my tongue in order not to respond, "Just because you haven't read any evidence, doesn't mean it doesn't exist!" Given that hospital food isn't the most appetizing to begin with, I was grateful that Robert and Kirsten were willing to make food runs for me—Noorish Restaurant on 109th Street was my favourite. One night while still in the hospital, my bestie Nat called SkipTheDishes and had dinner delivered to us from Noorish; now *that* was a treat!

During early morning rounds, one of the resident doctors who was part of the Neurosurgical team came to deliver my results. He confirmed the presence of an inoperable tumour that the radiologist highly suspected of being a Glioblastoma Multiforme or other high-grade glioma. My sis asked if we could see it on the monitor and he agreed; I'll readily admit, seeing it was a shocker! At the time, there were two lobules centered within the left cingulate gyrus (helps process emotional experience, and to regulate behaviour and pain); the posterior lobe was slightly larger, measuring 2.3 cm x 2.9 cm x 3.2 cm. The anterior lobe measured 2.2 cm x 2.1 cm x 2.2 cm. There showed compression and invasion in the body of the corpus callosum and the tumour extended across the midline from left to right by up to 1.5 cm, compressing the right cingulate gyrus. No wonder I had been struggling to function!

After we were back in my room, leaving Robert and me to process the news, Kirsten excused herself to make the painful but necessary phone calls to our parents and to our younger sisters, Jocelyn and Melanie.

The nightmare that was the cramped hospital room continued for another day. Although I'd received a great deal of sympathy from the nurses on duty for what I was having to deal with, at the time there was no space for me to move. The next day, my roommate hosted one of his "friends", and their conversation was loud, ignorant, and crude. My twin sis would have none of it and asked them to please watch their mouths. They apologized and were marginally better. However, this "friend" had gone shopping and picked up some Axe body spray, which he decided to spray in copious amounts. My twin sis went into full defence mode then, understandably angry, and explained quite clearly that firstly, they were breaking the hospital's scent-free rule, and secondly, that I was hypersensitive to scents, especially given that I had a brain tumour. They were chastened, but she was done with them. She marched out into the hallway to make a formal complaint to the staff on duty.

But it was truly the next occurrence that cemented my move to a room across the hall. As a quadriplegic, my roommate had no control over his bowels, and after soiling the bed the stench of his excrement put me over the edge. We waited in the hallway for at least two hours while staff cleaned him and his bedding. My sister insisted that we be moved, and my husband, who had been out but returned to hear of this latest event—furious—agreed. By late in the day, we were moved to a triple room across the hallway. Fortunately, I had the bed closest to the window and nearest the washroom! It was divine in comparison to what I'd suffered through the previous two nights. I remained there for the duration of my stay at UAH.

Kirsten also pressed the issue of my getting a biopsy sooner regardless of my lack of major symptoms: i.e. I was in no pain nor did I have any headaches. I remained in a blissed-out state. She was still unconvinced that my neurosurgeon was the right fit, so we had an agreement that she would meet with the neurosurgery team prior to my biopsy. Kirsten's law practice involves reading clinical records and she has interacted with medical specialists, including neurosurgeons, in consultation and at trial. "It's a good thing you don't get easily intimidated!" said one of my former high school students to her after hearing about this interview, which was comprised of the neurosurgeon, one of his chief residents, his neurosurgical physician's assistant, and the charge nurse of Neurosurgery. They met for about twenty minutes during which Kirsten was able to ask all of her questions, at times expressing herself frankly and with considerable grief and emotion. Each question was respectfully addressed and thoroughly responded to. The neurosurgeon shared his pragmatically direct prognosis, which Kirsten had recently shared with me. However shocking, through this somewhat cathartic discussion, Kirsten was left feeling more confident about him performing the procedure. She pressed the team to expedite the biopsy and they agreed they would. The renowned-to-be-gruff and perfunctory senior neurosurgeon even hugged Kirsten at the end of the meeting!

Given Kirsten's efforts advocating for me, the biopsy was scheduled within thirty-six hours. The night before, a resident came into my room to explain how the procedure would go and had me sign the consent form. It was quite late at night, which meant that Kirsten and Robert were not in attendance and I was fairly dopey on my latest dose of dexamethasone. The resident actually explained the wrong procedure, which registered in my muddled mind as such. I didn't say anything at the time because I trusted that the correct steps would in fact be taken at the time of the biopsy. Sleep was fitful at best, as I had a partial view from my window of the gigantic STARS helicopter landing and taking off. This is the emergency helicopter transport system in Alberta, and its use is a gift that saves lives, but is only used in extreme emergencies where time is of the utmost essence. As an empath, I was quite disturbed by the frequency of hearing the incredibly loud whirring of the blades and what that sound represented. I got into the habit of sending up a prayer of "Bless, bless, bless" each time I heard the deafening whirring of the blades.

Early the next morning, a different resident arrived to apologize on behalf of the medical team and to explain the correct biopsy procedure and sign a new consent form. Robert and Kirsten arrived *just* as I was being wheeled out for my biopsy. They kissed me and said that they'd see me soon. They nervously waited for me in the stunningly beautiful Guru Nanak Healing Garden, a peaceful oasis within the walls of the University of Alberta Hospital. I have a blurry recollection of being wheeled into the neurosurgery waiting room, where I was one of at least four others. There were at least three kind folks who shared with me once again how things were going to happen once I was under anaesthetic. I was without fear and possessed total trust that I would be well cared for. I remember the bright lights, the mask being placed over my nose and mouth, and then nothing until I was rather forcefully awoken from my anaesthetic. I'd been content to stay under as I was having some lovely dreams. Apparently, there was some initial worry as my temperature had dropped rather dramatically, but I was totally fine, and blearily greeted the medical staff that welcomed me back to consciousness. I was wheeled back to my room where Kirst and Robert waited. I was able to rest quietly, interrupted on occasion by the nursing staff who had to repeatedly take my blood pressure and administer my dexamethasone.

Let the Healing Begin

Kirst showed me a photo she had taken of a poster of a monthly offering at the UAH of a free Healing Sound Bath. The poster featured a gong, a harmonium, an Indigenous drum, and several Tibetan Singing Bowls and Crystal Healing Bowls. As it happened, the next Healing Sound Bath was to take place the day after my biopsy! It was certainly something to look forward to while we waited to hear the results, which could take time. The following day, Kirst escorted me down to the ground floor, to UAH's McMullen Art Gallery where the Healing Sound Bath would be taking place. We arrived several minutes early, and I—sporting the latest in hospital gown fashion, with my sweatpants over top—made myself comfortable, introducing myself to the musician, Sparrow. It turned out to be a transformational experience. I recollect having Sparrow ground us with the traditional drum, feeling the vibrations of it over my head and body; it was so powerful! She played the bowls and I woke up sobbing to the sound of her melodious voice singing the words from the chorus of "Love Can Build a Bridge" by The Judds, which asks, "don't you think it's time?"

I didn't consciously recognize why I was sobbing so hard except that on some level it felt like a recognition that I was in receipt of an answer—it *was* time to build that bridge to heal myself! It was a musical and spiritual affirmation of the videos I watched on Gaia.com on Heart-Brain Coherence! I have since added that song to my "Healing Journey" Spotify playlist.

With Kirsten's advocacy, two days after my biopsy, we received the news that my brain tumour was in fact a Grade IV Glioblastoma Multiforme. This didn't really mean much to me as at the time I didn't have any particular interest in knowing what type of tumour it was. When asked if I wished to hear my prognosis, I categorically refused. It was of *no* interest to me! To this day, I maintain that I am not my diagnosis nor my prognosis. The medical team didn't know me and my capabilities. How could they judge how long I had left to walk this Earth? Once the diagnosis had been confirmed, the chief neurosurgeon shared the prognosis with Kirsten in a private conversation. When she and Robert were out for dinner at Earls she asked if he wished to know the prognosis. They were devastated and heartbroken but attempted to put on brave faces. I remained convinced that I would be fine, and this was an energetic brain injury that I would be able to heal through my readily accessible toolbox of seemingly random skills that I'd gathered and honed over my adulthood.

I posted on Facebook what in hindsight was a rather naive, tongue-in-cheek update bluntly stating: "I have issues with my tissues! I have a Grade IV Glioblastoma Multiforme buried deep in my brain!" (With no grasp whatsoever as to the effect of this statement on other people, I was taken aback by their panicked and shocked responses.) It was only later once I had better clarity, that I realized that I could have cushioned my statement using more gentle language. After all, I knew there had been something in my brain back in February, but no one else did!

Chapter 5

Shi(f)t Happens

INTERESTINGLY, WHEN IT came time to be discharged from the University hospital, I found myself a bit reluctant to go as I'd gotten comfortable with the level of care I'd been receiving from the nurses. Robert had been working hard behind the scenes to arrange housing for us, in consultation with Kirst. It was going to be within walking distance to the Cross Cancer Institute and have ready access to the hospital. I soon learned that he'd arranged for us to stay in the Galen Lofts, directly across the street from the hospital. Ours was going to be a corner loft on the third floor: unit 303; however, we were unable to move in until three nights after being discharged.

Notice the repetition of the number three? I am fascinated with numerology, specifically the type used in Kundalini Yoga often referred to as Tantric Numerology. I don't have as thorough a background in it as I'd like, but it was part of my Kundalini Yoga Teacher Training. Tantric Numerology is based on the understanding that we as human beings are comprised of Ten Light Energy Bodies. These consist of the Soul Body, three aspects of the mind (Positive, Negative, Neutral), the physical vehicle that houses all of the Light Energy Bodies, which include not only the Soul but the Arc line (aka the "Halo"), the Pranic body, the Aura, and the Radiant Body. There is a fair amount of information available on the Ten Bodies on the internet; specifically, the 3HO Foundation website offers much in the way of simple descriptions. In a nutshell, the number three represents the Positive Mind, that aspect of the mind that when functioning well, sees the blessings and benefits of one's choices. It is solution oriented. It just so happened that using the tantric numerological formula, 2019 is a "3" as well $(2 + 0 + 1 + 9 = 12; 1 + 2 = 3)$. I felt like that because we were in a year representing the Positive Mind, that at least partially explained why I was able to be so trusting that all that was going down was part of a grander plan for me. I used my understanding of the tantric numerological symbolism in the coming months to choose my lockers at CCI, typically choosing 6 (Arc line/Halo) or 7 (Aura) when I had to go for radiation.

As someone who'd been traumatized by their Grade 6 Math Teacher calling them "stupid" in front of the whole class, and hearing from their well-intentioned mother, "I don't get why you don't get this; it's easy!", when it came to math homework, I'd grown up with a core belief that I was "no good with numbers". I have since learned otherwise, but only through this healing journey of mine. I "see" numbers symbolically and in terms of patterns; that would explain my artistic fascination with mandalas over the past several years!

From Hospital to Outpatient Dorm

Because I was unable to move into what would be my home for two months for three days after being discharged from the hospital, Kirsten and Robert had arranged for me to stay in the adjoining Outpatient Residence. OAR, as it is referred to, is an old 1970s building that hadn't had much work done to it since. My understanding is that it used to be where the nurses stayed when doing their training.

Packing up my hospital room was a bit of a whirlwind. I had to change into normal clothing for the first time in about a week. Just as we had checked out and left the neurosurgery wing, dear friends Jeff and Joanne Granberg arrived with gifts in hand. Jeff and Robert go back fifty years in friendship. We sat together and visited for a while at one of the tables outside of the neurosurgery wing and I was feeling quite discombobulated, downright spacey. But I was grateful for their visit and their gifts of pajamas and slippers, and their assistance transporting my luggage through the maze of hallways connecting the hospital to the OAR.

My room in OAR was reminiscent of a university dorm room. As my senses were still in overdrive, the huge bouquet that had been given to me from Kirsten's law firm was left in the common area, as the smell of the lilies was overpowering in the confined space. What was very sweet is that after leaving them, we came into the common area a few hours later to find that the custodian had divided up the bouquet into several smaller jars and vases and placed flowers on each of the tables and in the living room.

Robert was departing that same day to return to Yellowknife for three days, returning the morning that we'd be able to move into the loft. He was reluctant to go, but we needed him to go home to deal with our dogs, who were clueless as to why their "parents" were away. Our incredible neighbours, Ray and Denise Halwas, who have a dog of their own, initially took in our two pooches, followed by cherished friends Tim Mercer, Debbie Meade, and their aspiring vet daughter, Shannon.

Kirsten stayed with me in the dorm that first night and I didn't get much sleep. Dear friends of Kirsten had called her that night to get the scoop as to what was going on and to commiserate as their elderly father died of the same brain cancer. Because she was on the bed beside mine, I overheard her describe my brain tumour as inoperable. Oddly, that was the first I had heard that term and I had a visceral reaction to its use. It took a very conscious and consistent effort to do what I called a "mental reframe" of the term. I began to mentally chant, "I have an energetic brain injury; I will heal" over and over again.

I was also very preoccupied with Mom's anticipated arrival the next day and the fact that she (too) is a light sleeper. The excessive heat in the room despite the open window, and the all-night noise of the LRT station were all quite overwhelming for me. From 1:00 am until at least 4:00 am, they were cleaning the tracks. To me it was deafening, despite wearing headphones. Exhausted on all levels, Kirsten slept through it all as she was wise enough to be wearing heavy-duty earplugs. I did eventually doze off, having listened to one of the Yoga Nidra scripts on Insight Timer that became one of my go-to recordings: "Yoga Nidra for a Grateful Heart", by Maria McDonald. I listened to it daily for weeks and still do on occasion, particularly when I feel like I need to tap into gratitude. My sleep was fitful and quite irregular. Certainly, however, in the early days of March, I was often asked about my sleep. To the well-intentioned questions I developed the response: "I got the rest that I required, thank you." At that point I was doing two, forty-minute Yoga Nidra scripts through the night, so I was getting the rest that I required as that's like getting the equivalent of four hours of sleep per script.

I started getting phone calls from the Cross Cancer Institute (CCI) the first full day in the dorm. I was alone at the time, as Kirsten was picking Mom up at the airport. I was alone and struggling to process and write down the information of my initial appointments. My handwriting was almost illegible but I somehow managed. There were at least three different phone calls, each describing different appointments and the process of what I'd need to do over three days. For certain, it was information overload for my poor brain, and I struggled to recite to Kirsten, Mom, and later Robert the details of each of the calls.

Kirsten brought Mom immediately to OAR and up to my room. We tearfully embraced for a long time. She arrived with a bucket-load of cards and thoughtful gifts, such as a hand-knit prayer shawl from a dear family friend whom I still call "Aunt" despite not being a blood relative. I napped and rested for a few hours, while Mom and Kirst went to the common area to talk and cry together. They also watched the documentary *HEAL* on Kirst's iPad, which made Mom feel much better afterwards.

Mom read and did crosswords for a while after crawling into bed, eventually falling asleep in the midst, exhausted from her long day of travel. I turned out the bedside lamp and attempted to rest. I stuck my headphones on, listening to my first of several playlists I created over the coming days and weeks on Spotify. This particular playlist is called "Mo's Meditation Mix" and I found it exceptionally helpful then to put me into a meditative state of mind. One song, a forty-five-minute piece called "This Universe" by Singh Kaur is transcendental! It is in both English and Gurmukhi, the sacred ancient language of the Sikhs, and the mantra used in this song is one of protection: "Aad Guray Nameh, Jugaad Guray Nameh, Sat Guray Nameh, Siri Guru Devay Nameh", and is called the Mangala Charan mantra within the tradition of Kundalini Yoga. It refers to the acknowledgement and honouring of the primal wisdom, the wisdom through the ages, the true wisdom, and the great unseen wisdom. When chanted regularly, it opens one up to receive guidance and protection and to dispel all doubts. But it was the English lyrics that truly drew me in, as they seemed to echo my ultimate beliefs:

> To the one who meditates upon perfect peace
> All pain and sorrow depart
> Meditate upon Who contains this Universe
> Whose Holy Name is the whisper on the lips
> Of the Entire Creation

Over the next several weeks, I would put this song on repeat and listen to it for hours, as it brought me great comfort. That second night in the OAR, however, sleep remained elusive, so I did a forty-minute practice of Yoga Nidra to get the rest I required, and then another also by Maria McDonald called "Yoga Nidra for Wholeness and Connection" on Insight Timer. I don't remember falling asleep but did at the very least enter an altered state of consciousness, one that I had never previously nor since experienced.

"Spiritual Orgasm"

Frankly, I'm unable to find words to adequately describe what happened in those early morning hours, except to say that imagine the absolute best orgasm you have ever experienced and multiply it exponentially. I wasn't awake, nor was I asleep. I was overtaken by pure sensation. The powerful waves of energy began in my root, through my groin and pelvis, rushing up like a tidal wave through my torso, causing my arms to fly up into the air and remain there for at least a minute. The energy continued through my hands and fingers, up into my neck up into and out of the crown of my head. Simultaneously, a voice that I could hear and feel but didn't recognize as my own starting from deep within my core; sounding a bit like an untrained singer experimenting with opera, getting progressively louder until it was like an ecstatic scream. I felt like I was being lifted off the bed. With my arms still involuntarily suspended in the air overhead, I heard myself saying repeatedly, "I'm in bliss! I'm in bliss! I feel no pain! I have no fear!" It was my Soul's Call being set free. If you've ever seen Michelangelo's "St. Teresa of Avila" sculpture with the angel's arrows piercing the heart of the saint, that's the visual I have typically used to describe what I underwent: pure and unadulterated ecstasy!

As you might imagine, Mom was terrified by what she was awoken to so suddenly and started to call out my pet-name in a panicked tone, "MAURN! MAURN! Wake up! Wake up!" I sat up as she turned on the bedside lamp, eventually able to lower my arms as I came into fuller consciousness. I was beaming, suffused with a lightness of being that I'd never before experienced. Meanwhile, Mom was crying, releasing the stress of the shock she'd received. I too began to sob, as it was only then that I came to the full recognition that I was unconditionally loved. The next day, she expressed her profound gratitude for having borne witness to my mystical encounter. Until that point, she hadn't realized just how profoundly at a soul level this healing was meant to be.

I elected to keep this experience relatively private until I could better process it, save for my twinnie, a couple of spiritually-oriented cousins with whom I had been in regular contact via text, and friends that I didn't think would think I'd gone off my rocker. Months later, I still feel like I'm processing the experience, yearning on some level to repeat it.

My younger sis, Jocelyn, her hubby Greg, and my seven-year-old niece drove up from Calgary that same day to visit. I understood their strong desire to assuage their shock at my condition, but I'll admit I was a bit concerned about the energy level of my niece. I was not sure how much I'd be able to tolerate this early on in my healing journey, which had truly just begun. Kirsten met them downstairs and guided them up to my room. My niece came running across the room for a much-desired hug and kiss. I was pretty spacey, so not entirely aware of my word choice as, in an attempt to make her feel better, I casually responded to one of her questions about my cancer diagnosis with, "Well, everyone has cancer cells in their bodies all the time!" Fortunately, she'd gotten distracted by something and somehow— thankfully—didn't hear my response. My sister and brother-in-law did, though, and were rather appalled that I'd say this to my young niece. I was quite oblivious at the time thanks to the dose of dexamethasone I'd recently taken, but later realized that my response could have been more age appropriate. Thankfully, it had been decided that my niece would come in, share with me the beautiful card she'd painted for her Auntie Mo-Mo but soon after, Kirst would take her and give her a tour of the hospital's common areas while I visited with my "sissah Joce" and Greg.

Joce is renowned for her thoughtful gift-giving and this visit was no different. She'd put together a care package that included fruit and treats that I wouldn't have had access to in the hospital, as well as a hilarious Sloth Boomerang toy that she'd found at a dollar store. We each had a grand time pinging one another harmlessly with these soft plastic rubbery sloths. It was one way to lighten the atmosphere in the coming months whenever the atmosphere started to feel a bit heavy. Once my manual dexterity really started to return, I became quite accomplished at sending a sloth across the room in our loft! Once we moved into the loft, I kept the sloths and the boomerang as part of my corner altar, to balance out some more spiritually significant items.

Robert called that evening before we went out to dinner at Earls. I was able to tell him what had transpired with my ecstatic experience, but definitely wished to re-enact parts of it in person as best I could. He was understandably concerned. But at the same time he expressed that he was starting to believe in all this "miracle stuff" as he'd received a phone call from his ex-wife saying that he needed to come by the house because she had a gift for me! This was miraculous in the sense that in the twenty years that Robert and I had been together, there had been no relationship between her and me, which reinforced my core belief of unworthiness and insecurity. It was my turn to be shocked and quite moved. I thought, "Wow, this Forgiveness Decree really does create miracles!"

I got dressed to put on the many layers required to not freeze on the short two-block walk to the restaurant with my mom and twinnie. Winter was definitely still present in the capital city in early March, and I was grateful that Robert was going to be bringing additional warm layers for me when he arrived the next morning. We found comfortable seating on the lounge side of Earls and because of my heightened sensitivities to everything, I sat with my back towards the television screens and the majority of the people in the restaurant. I kept my food order simple: steak, asparagus, and salad with club soda. Before we left, an anonymous text message came through: "Hey Maureen, I'm sorry it's taken me so long to write to you. Honestly, I'm at a loss of [sic] words how sorry I am that all of this is happening. I've been really struggling since hearing the news and I can't even imagine how scary this all is but I just wanted to say that I know how strong you are and how strong spirited you are and that I'm sending every ounce of love and positive vibes I have your way." I read the text to Mom and Kirst and said, "Who do you think sent this?" as it came up with just the phone number, and no contact name. It was such a beautiful, heartfelt sentiment that a part of me was thinking, "I should know who wrote this!" I suspected that it may have been my stepson Jacob, identical twin of Aidan who I'd heard from the previous weekend, but I wasn't certain. Intriguingly, as I re-read the texts that each of them sent, I'm amazed at how similar the wording is, despite them not living in the same city. Plus, I still giggle as I reflect on how I chose to respond, despite not being certain who had written this most recent message!

"Hola! There is NO fear! I am pain-free actually and believe this is the next chapter in the journey of my soul. This is a powerfully healing experience for me. I feel incredibly trusting of the Wisdom of the Universe. P.S. I have NO idea who this is btw…. Please enlighten me!"

It was, in fact, Jacob, who apologized for not identifying himself initially and said he was glad to hear that and fully believed that too, hoping to see me soon. Mom, Kirst, and I all shared tears as it now truly felt like the miracles were happening. As someone whose primary Love Language is "Words of Affirmation", I was finally hearing the words I had longed to hear for twenty years.

Chapter 6

Healing Journey: Moving from Denial to Clarity

Home away from home

ROBERT RETURNED TO Edmonton on the first Sunday of March. He immediately drove to the Outpatient Residence to assist in getting me packed up and moved into the Galen Lofts. My husband is a goal-oriented fellow. I truly have never encountered someone so quickly efficient in getting things done; when he has a goal in mind, look out! And that goal was to get me to more comfortable "digs", where I would be living for the next eight weeks.

So on the third day of the third month of the year, we moved into a third floor corner loft: unit 303. We got ourselves moved in and unpacked. Kirsten and Mom assisted by going to the grocery store. For several years, I'd been educating myself on the food that best nourished me, and we were certainly fortunate to be able to afford to buy as many organic products as we did. This ranged not only from food items, but also cleaning products, including dish soap to hand soap to shampoo, conditioner, and body lotion. I maintain that it's not only what we put *in* our bodies, but what we put *on* our bodies that helps to nourish us; after all, our skin is the largest organ of the body.

The loft was incredibly comfortable with ample natural light as there were windows that ran from waist height all the way to the ceiling and ran the length and width of the loft. I immediately fell in love with my home-away-from-home. We rearranged the furniture to be more welcoming, adding my sheepskin and meditation cushion from home, so that I'd have a comfy seat for my meditations and the basic yoga postures that I was hoping to resume sooner rather than later. Kirsten and Mom showed up with a folding wooden TV table and footstool that they'd picked up especially for us, and which were most welcome additions. I'd also set up an ever-evolving "altar" in the corner of the living room on the wide window ledge. Some of the items included white Buffalo sage to cleanse the space, an oyster shell, a beeswax candle that I'd received as a gift, a shallow ceramic bowl that I'd asked Robert to bring from home in which I placed some crystals, and a fun glass "stone" that said "Enlighten Up!" Over time, different mala bracelets that I'd received as gifts were placed there at night, along with the gift of the sacred word: "namaste" in a copper-coloured metal from a dear friend and former neighbour from home. Another gift included a dry mounted sign based on a meme that I'd felt incredibly strongly about when it showed up on my Instagram feed. There was no credit given on the meme but after looking up the poem on the internet, I was at least able to find the name of the person, Munshira Althaf, who wrote the powerful words that continue to move me.

A second sign I had made up was based on the lyrics of the Judd's song's chorus of "Love Can Build a Bridge". Janet, owner of a Yellowknife graphic design shop, had designed the quote with a lovely teal-coloured outline of a mandala on a square background, with bold black letters and I leaned that one against one of the multiple windows in the living room.

The third sign arrived the next month, when my friend Debbie came to spend six days with me after Robert's return to Yellowknife. It's based on an acronym that one of my former Kundalini yoga students came up with for the sacred mantra within the Kundalini Yoga tradition: *Sat Nam*. Each letter represents one phase of my healing process:

Surrender
Allow
Truth
Now
Accept
Miracles

Sat Nam

We also made a trip to the fair-trade store, Ten Thousand Villages, where I picked up a shallow handwoven basket plus a number of picture frames that I intended to fill with images of people I considered to be part of my "healing tribe of sisters". I also found a really special wooden frame that had the word "Love" carved on it, in which I placed one of my favourite photos of my beloved stepson, Lukey, when he was about six years old, the age that I came into his life.

With regards to the next medical steps, we were left in limbo for a few days. We tried to get out each day, despite the cold. One such outing was to Whyte Avenue. I was like a fawn learning how to walk, as I'd lost a great deal of weight and muscle mass. Weak-kneed but thrilled to be out and about, I enjoyed some much-needed silly time with Kirsten as she invited me to sit on a child's plastic car, and she wheeled me around. We giggled like fools and got many of the folks around us smiling. Soon after, we joined my somewhat mortified husband and our smiling mother at the Starbucks inside Chapters.

To add routine to my days and allow me to feel a bit more in control, I developed rituals to follow in the morning and evening, based in traditional knowledge, such as smudging using the white Buffalo sage or Palo Santo to cleanse the space and myself; and Ayurvedic wisdom, in practicing a variation of Abhyanga (full body oil massage), oil pulling (a dental cleaning technique "slooshing" coconut oil around one's teeth for up to twenty minutes), and soaking my feet in cool water at night before bed to name but a few. These routines became a mainstay to feeling somewhat normal. I later incorporated what is known as "Ishnaan", a form of hydrotherapy which involves the application of the oil before taking a cold shower for as long as one could stand, rapidly massaging one's limbs and trunk, whilst wearing undershorts that insulated the genitals and thighs from the cold water. It's not a time to use soap and shampoo! It's fantastic for the strengthening of the immune system as well as improving circulation.

Energetic "Downloads" Begin

What I've come to refer to as "energetic downloads" or intuitive "hits" began the very first night in the Galen Lofts. My sleep remained sporadic but in the early morning hours I was awoken by a voice that told me, "You're going to speak at Grad." I found my journal and noted that. Speaking at Sir John Grad had been a dream of mine for many years; however, I *never* thought I had anything of importance to share! I was nervous and excited at the prospect, but still questioning what I had to share with the graduating class of 2019 and their families that could make a lasting impact. I had various topics racing through my brain before I eventually dropped off once more to sleep. Between 4:00 and 4:30 am, my mother's voice came through loud and clear to me, saying "Your sister's on fire!" She was staying with Kirsten at our cousin's house. I sat up with a jolt, retrieved my phone, and immediately texted Kirsten stating, "You're on fire," and went on asking how she was feeling and enquiring about the functioning of her digestive system (i.e. associated with the element of fire—our "digestive fire" as it were). She was awoken by my text and not at all impressed but simultaneously concerned; she responded that her "tummy is good", thank you very much, but she felt the need to do more exercise due to her back pain. (Note: It was later that I realized Mom's voice was actually meant to be communicating that *I* was "on fire", as I'd moved into a manic phase due to taking too much of my prescribed bioidentical thyroid hormone replacement.)

I had a rather wild session with Jillian and the Record Keepers where the energy generated by her use of Light Languages and resulting "energetic surgery" was palpable. Systematically, they went through various organs and energy centres, spending a good deal of time on my gut, my heart, and my brain specifically. I could *really* feel the work being done in my brain; my whole head vibrated. My headphones often crackled, cutting in and out, and behind my closed eyes, I would see bright colours flash: red, orange, yellow, and sometimes violet. It was a bit unnerving at the time, but I reassured myself that it was all helping me to heal. Part of what I find fascinating in my healing work with Jillian and the Record Keepers is that I've been able to reintroduce foods into my diet that I have not been able to for over thirty years! After that session, I was given homework. I was asked to start paying particular attention to the wisdom experienced in my body—the messages coming through—and act upon this wisdom. As it turns out, the wisdom in my body seems to be strongly connected to the Five Great Elements: Earth, Fire, Water, Air, and Ether/Space.

The next energetic download again came through my hearing in a voice stridently calling me to "Clear the Air!" Doing my best not to wake my husband lying beside me, I got up and immediately went to the kitchen window in an attempt to open it. Meeting a lot of resistance, I then shifted to one of the living room windows, again failing to budge the window. At that point, my husband questioned "**What** are you doing?" to which I responded loudly "I'm CLEARING the AIR!" Since he was awake, I went into the bedroom, and the window flew open with no resistance. I stuck my head out breathing deeply the freshly crisp and cold air until I could feel the shift in energy in our loft. Only then did I close the window. But I didn't immediately return to bed because I knew that the literal clearing of the air wasn't sufficient. I also needed to metaphorically clear the air through writing. Interestingly, in the days leading up to this download to clear the air, I'd been feeling a stuffiness and staleness in the air and wrote it off to smudging without opening a window afterwards due to the cold. It was only after sitting to write for more than two hours that I finally felt the energy shift more completely. I posted on Facebook my first of several timeline updates to come clean about what I'd been in such denial of in terms of the extreme and rapid deterioration of my health. Posting allowed me to tap into my vulnerability, confessing to things like early symptoms that now seemed so obvious to me in hindsight. It was humbling and incredibly liberating.

There were additional and regular downloads over the coming days, all revolving around the elements. I would be awoken, typically in the early morning hours, by a voice telling me to run the tub and soak in it. Also relating to the water element, I was also encouraged to better "Go with the flow" or "Hydrate". I was drinking a lot of water and tea at that point, oftentimes consuming up to or over three litres a day. I was flushing my system. Additionally, I got a regular sensation in my mouth when it was time to "lubricate" versus "hydrate". I would get up no matter the time, also typically in the very early morning hours to make myself a "Golden Milk", a "cure-all" beverage within the tradition of Ayurveda. Traditionally this beverage consists of ghee (clarified butter). I would use coconut oil as I don't tolerate most forms of cow dairy, not even clarified, turmeric cooked in the oil/ghee, a cup of milk of choice, ginger, cinnamon, and often some ground pepper all heated on the stove top and then sweetened to taste, typically with honey but maple syrup also works. I would often add a pinch of nutmeg and sometimes cardamom too, making it more of a "Moon Mylk". At times I would also add a teaspoon of maca powder to balance my hormones and ashwagandha powder as an adaptogenic herb for my body to adapt to the stress it was under.

At this point, I seemed to be spending a lot of my energetic focus volleying between the air and water elements, but it wasn't long before my fiery manic phase took over. One evening after Robert and I had discussed and agreed that we would pay the rent for Mom and Dad to have a loft on the floor beneath us, we approached Mom with our plan. Mom did her best to refuse, tapping into her oft-adopted "martyr" role, which had driven me crazy for years. I would take it no longer. I went into full-on "Loyal Lioness" mode and was literally in Mom's face shaking my finger and screaming at her: "Don't you know that Robert and I would do anything to protect and support my family? You do not have the right to turn us down! I refuse to allow you to say no!" She sat as far back in her armchair as she possibly could, looking rather afraid, and meekly responded: "I think I liked you better before." She reluctantly capitulated, and thankfully, we can laugh about this situation now.

The following day, I exploded for some reason at my husband in front of my mom and Kirsten in that first week at the loft. Recognizing I was "off", I crawled into bed, intentionally lying on my right side in a restorative yoga pose called "Side-Lying Savasana", so that my left nostril was facing up. This position is associated with creating calm in the nervous system, which I desperately needed. That way the breath would naturally shift predominantly to the left nostril and I would relax. I played some beautifully peaceful music by Ashana to aid in creating calm, while Robert left to go spend time with a long-time friend of his, and Mom and Kirst hung out in the living room of the loft. Soon after I settled, I called out to them, "Am I being obnoxious?" to which they very kindly responded, "No, but you're being aggressive, and could be kinder to your husband. He's feeling completely overwhelmed." I agreed wholeheartedly, and feeling chastened, I sent him a text acknowledging that I recognized he was struggling and committed to being more kind. After all, the sense of overwhelm and panic was entirely natural. But because I knew at an intrinsic level, I would be fine, I just couldn't wrap my head around how those around me were struggling so. *I would be fine, truly.* And I naively felt that all he and the rest of my family needed to do was to trust more. Trust that there was a higher power at work and that the Universe had a grander plan for me, with healing myself in order to more readily access my gifts being part of said plan.

After my rest, Mom, Kirst, and I walked through a winter wonderland to get to Noorish, where I treated them to dinner. The walk there and back felt a bit like Mother Nature's last hurrah, and we loved the snow and the nature therapy. I made a conscious effort to remain quiet and let Kirsten fill us in on the renovations that were happening at her townhouse as well as the VIP opportunity of meeting and greeting Michelle Obama in Vancouver the following week. Mom also regaled Kirst and me with stories of her and Dad's courtship and early relationship. Summary: it was quick and very romantic! It was such a precious time that all three of us treasured, as there was so much laughter and so much love. The walk back to the loft was riddled with giggles, especially when Kirsten pretended to go climb a tree.

Medical Appointment Mania

At my intake to Cross Cancer Institute, I was given an ID card that I would need to present at each appointment I attended. Kirsten and Robert accompanied me. We first met with the nurse who asked me to fill in paperwork which I deferred to Robert as I wasn't able to write at that point. He also weighed me, and I was down twenty pounds from my normal weight. We were joined by the Radiation Oncologist and one of his residents. He explained the radiation. Kirsten recorded notes, as I was on edge, being full-on manic. The oncologist also said that I would have a decision to make regarding whether or not I wanted to be part of a clinical trial, which would be eight weeks instead of six weeks of radiation. I declined. Dr. Amanie also detailed the possible side effects which didn't faze me at all. He described the radiation mask with which I would be fitted the following day.

Dr. Jay Easaw was the chemotherapy oncologist assigned to my case and he joined Dr. Amanie. Despite my symptoms, I was immediately taken with how good looking the man was, which made me giggle. But my giggling soon turned to an "in your face" attitude when he and Dr. Amanie continued to refer to my "treatment plan" and not as I was calling it: a "healing journey", and what I'd been calling "Integrated Medicine" as "Alternative Medicine". At one point, Dr. Easaw stopped me mid-tirade to say, "Maureen, we'll call it anything you'd like, but just know that we are all on the same side. Our top priority is to see you healed! You'll be the one making all of the final decisions. All we ask is that no matter what you are choosing to explore, you are up front and entirely truthful with us." I appreciated his willingness to put me in charge of my own health.

The pharmacist talked about the specific drugs I'd be taking for my chemo, which wasn't only the chemo itself but also an antiemetic and an antibiotic. I felt incredibly fortunate that my team were all on the same page as I was. They were open to my exploring the integrative route provided I was entirely honest with them.

Dr. Easaw wished to add one more blood test. He recognized my manic state as being indicative of too much thyroid medication.

This lab was mainly to get a baseline for the weekly labs I'd do commencing soon. Once done, Robert, Kirsten, and I walked back to the loft, where I needed some food and grounding exercises. I began to intentionally shake—I believe it's referred to as "primal shaking"— like what animals instinctively do after escaping a predator to rid themselves of the excess adrenaline and cortisol in their sympathetic nervous systems. I shook and bounced my way to calm. I also needed to lie down once I was fed and feeling more relaxed.

Getting fitted for the radiation mask the next day was a key component to my decision to approach everything from a place of curious fascination. I chose that morning to wear a pair of lime green jeans and a white top. Green is related to healing and is the colour associated with the heart chakra; wearing white automatically expands one's aura or electromagnetic field, Plus, white light is a combination of all colours of the visible spectrum. Just for fun, I sported a pair of fuzzy pink and red socks with the word "Hot" and an image of a tamale pepper on each of them. They not only made me laugh, but when I went into the room, the young radiation techs also got a huge kick out of the socks. I mentioned how good the warm malleable mask felt being "massaged" and fitted to my face, saying it felt like I was receiving a facial. I asked them if they also did manicures and pedicures. I don't think they were accustomed to someone so cheery and fearless as I was through the potentially nerve-wracking process.

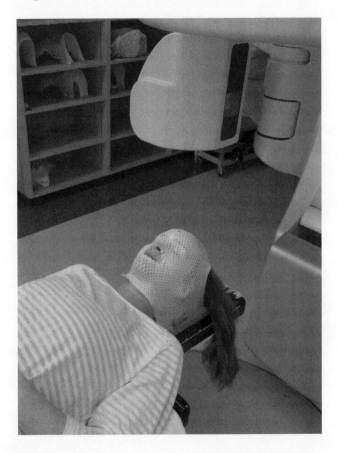

Once my mask hardened, I got an MRI that would measure where the gamma rays would enter my brain. There would be three rays in total once I began my protocol. The process that day was fascinating; I felt surprisingly safe and "locked in" and fortunately not at all claustrophobic. It was on that day that my MRI indicated that my tumour had increased in volume from just over 45 cubic centimeters to just shy of 57; it was growing quickly!

Friends like Family

My actual six-week protocol wasn't scheduled to begin until later in March. Thus, with the weekend ahead of us and a special visitor arriving in the wee hours of Saturday morning, we looked forward to spending time with one of my besties, Lisa Yang. A medical doctor with TCM training based in New Brunswick in the town where I grew up, Lisa was making a very quick "emergency" trip to visit, flying up from Atlanta, GA, where she'd been attending an essential oils leadership conference. She recognized and respected my initial reticence to incorporating brand-specific essential oils. It was over the coming days that I came to the realization of why I was so avoidant; it took a great deal of reflection on past choices and behaviours regarding branding.

Dean, the principal from the high school in Yellowknife where I taught since 1992 arrived, bearing a few thoughtful gifts and cards signed by the majority of my coworkers. I asked Dean to record a video message for staff which we had an absolute blast recording because it featured Kirst and I attempting to "floss" to Earth, Wind & Fire's "Let's Groove Tonight" and Justin Timberlake's "Can't Stop the Feeling".

It was right around this time that I made the deliberate decision to find time each day to dance. Sometimes it took convincing to get others to join me, but oftentimes they were up for the light-hearted fun. Other times still, I danced alone, happy to have the entire loft space to really let loose! The tunes varied though all had very positive lyrics. Over time, I built a "BT Dance Playlist" (BT is my tongue-in-cheek acronym for Brain Tumour) on Spotify that features some of my perpetual go-to songs for an affirming, energizing, gratitude-building way to inject joy into my day. Several songs from the group Aykanna's *Classics* album are featured on my playlist: "Beautiful Day" was literally the way I started my days in March, April, and beyond. One can't *not* be grateful when bopping along with that song! "Be the Light" and "Funky Divinity" became additional faves. I just love the lyrics in the latter when they say, "The moment has arrived, for you to be the gift you came to be!" and "It's time to be the gift that uplifts!" and to "Be that pipeline between Heaven and Earth!" There is also a popular Kundalini Meditation mantra within the song: "Ang Sang Wahe Guru" which is later translated in the song as, "Live in ecstasy of the Universe, Dances within every cell of my body." Sukhdev Jackson, the female lead of this husband and wife musical duo, reached out to me, saying "I bow to you and honor you and all that you are completing in this powerful lifetime. How divine you have discovered the gift of Spirit in your life."

Another go-to on my playlist was "Hymn of Healing" by Beautiful Chorus. The words resonated with me and I often played it on repeat:

I am a radiant being
Of light and healing
I feel peace, I am safe
I heal from a whole place

My friend and mentor, Dev Suroop Kaur reached out to let me know how she had chosen to deal with my situation: she was inspired to return to the recording studio to create a thirty-one-minute traditional version of the "Siri Gaitri Mantra". Commonly known as "Ra Ma Da Sa", it is the most popular healing mantra within the tradition of Kundalini Yoga, popularized by such beautiful voices as Snatam Kaur and Jai-Jagdeesh Kaur and more recently, Ajeet Kaur. Calling upon the energies of the Sun (Ra), the Moon (Ma), the Earth (Da) and Infinity (Sa), chanting this mantra acknowledges that we in fact already have all of these within us. I'd been listening to these various versions of this mantra for hours on end while in hospital and once discharged. I was overjoyed at the prospect of Dev Suroop's gesture, and we maintained a steady conversation over Messenger at various stages of the recording process. The recording is currently available on Bandcamp, Spotify, and Apple Music, with a portion of the proceeds going to the Brain Tumor Foundation of America.

Chapter 7

One Journey, Many Paths

Striving for Growth Towards Balance

I WAS STILL NOT sleeping a great deal. Many of my waking hours at night were spent in contemplation or practicing Yoga Nidra. It was during this time of intense reflection that I came to the realization that I was first challenged about what I believed made me "tick" several years ago. When a friend and colleague who was helping me model the "focusing interview" technique as part of the *Career Focusing*™ module of the CALM course to my students questioned my use of the word "striving", I'd been quite insistent that all my life my *raison d'être* was "Striving for Growth Towards Balance". I had to push, push, push to learn as much as I could about what would make me the absolute best version of myself: continually growing and simultaneously becoming better balanced. Over my adult years, my skill set grew varied and I took great pride in sharing my knowledge with as many folks as were open to receiving it. During my contemplation, I realized that my striving so hard was in fact, part of what made me sick to begin with. I was trying to be everything to everyone! My friend had intuited that I was pushing myself too hard. Additionally, I came to truly appreciate the purpose of acquiring all of the skills over the years in the form of various styles of yoga, meditation, studying Ayurveda, holistic nutrition, Emotional Freedom Technique, exploring different artistic expressions, and more! Each of these would serve to help *me* heal. No more were these seemingly random tidbits I'd picked up over the years to share with others; it was time to focus on myself.

So, if "Striving for Growth Towards Balance" wasn't what I was all about, what was? What gave me a passion to get up in the morning and live life to the fullest? I was definitely a driven person, but for the wrong reasons. Balance on all levels is a priority to me, but in my striving, in my searching, I'd become unbalanced because I was giving too much of myself away.

Over the weekend spent with my dear friend Lisa, I came to understand that I did not subscribe to the idea that there was only one right answer or one right path. Having never bought into that idea, as an adult I elected not to follow any one organized religion, though I'd grown up in the traditions of the relatively liberal United Church of Canada and remain fascinated with rituals from various traditions. I believe there is a higher organizing power and believe one can call it whatever works for oneself, whether it's God, Allah, Creator, Yahweh, Spirit, Source, Universe, or The Field. I don't limit myself to one term. I believe that we are spiritual beings embodied in a physical vehicle to transport us through this lifetime that we have chosen this time 'round. To the core of my being, I believe there are many paths to follow, but only *one* journey that is unique to each individual who inhabits a physical body. This journey will be influenced by all of a person's choices, actions, and even thoughts.

As I live near the shore of one of the world's largest lakes, and since realizing what makes me "tick" is what I have decided to call "One Journey, Many Paths", I like to verbally illustrate how the journey can be at times choppy and rough in stormy conditions—during disagreements in relationships for example—and in other times, smooth sailing. A person may have to pull into a bay for shelter until the proverbial storm passes or may float down a river channel for a change of scenery. They may believe they are taking the correct route, but in fact are on a bit of a detour and need to problem-solve their way back to their destination. This is so much easier said than done, isn't it? As someone who still struggles with wanting my husband to make healthier choices, I need to remind myself of my own advice on a regular basis.

So how does all of this relate to my reticence to commit to using a particular brand of essential oils over another? I realized that for me, quality is essential, but is not brand-specific. Not even as a teenager, when brand names seemed to be the "be all and end all", did I want to be seen sporting one particular brand over another. I just didn't buy into the whole "brand-name" superiority. Ever.

That said, by the end of her time with me, I was convinced by Lisa that in fact what she was asking me to do was to use what is likely the best-researched and scientifically based brand of essential oils on the market today. Yes, it's an MLM company, but it does an impressive amount of good in the world too, what with their "Helping Hands" initiative, their research, and use of ethical and sustainable sources, etc. Part of what Lisa set me up with before her departure was a "brain cancer protocol" for topical application and diffusion of essential oils. She made up a roller-ball blend and left me the oil bottles so that I could continue making the blends when I needed to. Fifteen drops of frankincense combined with five drops of cloves, diffused for thirty minutes, three times a day. For the roller ball blend, I use ten drops of frankincense, four drops of cloves and four drops of myrrh topped up with fractionated coconut oil in a ten-ml glass roller ball tube. I apply this blend from tailbone to brain stem along my spine ideally three times per day.

Lisa also set me up with gel caps of a proprietary supplement blend called DDR Prime™ As agreed with my team at CCI, I presented them with the documents describing the ingredients and researched benefits of the products to gain their approval before beginning the essential oil regime. I was incredibly grateful when the head pharmacist didn't anticipate they would interact poorly with any of the drugs he prescribed.

Reconnections

March 10th is a special day in our lives as it marks the anniversary of my younger sister's survival of a massive stroke at the age of thirty-eight. We touched base with Jocelyn over Kirst's phone via FaceTime, and we then ventured out on a road trip to Castor, Alberta, where much of Robert's family lives. Though Robert's strong desire was to drive through Camrose to continue on to Stettler and then Castor, to his great irritation, I insisted that we stop so that I could stretch my legs and use the washroom. I complained to Lisa about Robert being all about the destination and not about the journey—almost the polar opposite to me.

Thankfully, it had been decided in a couple of conversations with my sister-in-law, Kathy, that we would be limiting the numbers in the planned luncheon so as to not overwhelm me. We drove to what is fondly referred to as the "Grouse House", a gorgeous loft atop a garage space where Kathy now lives after the untimely death of her husband, Richard. Built by our nephew, Ian also transformed the garage at the "Grouse House" to a gorgeous, peaceful yoga studio.

I completely adore Robert's family, and I was thrilled to immerse myself in their fully expressed unconditional love. They are a very demonstrative family, tending to be on the enthusiastically vocal side, wonderfully so. There were *so* many questions! They were really struggling to comprehend how I could not have felt their love. I did my best to explain that it wasn't so much that I couldn't feel it; I knew they loved me. I just mistakenly felt that over the years there was *always* an unspoken comparison happening between myself and my husband's ex-wife and that somehow, I never measured up: a recurring theme in my life.

The luncheon itself was nourishing to body, mind, and soul—and particularly heart, for *all* of us. All of the food provided was from the gardens of my sisters-in-law, my nephew Ian and his wife Dana's *RedTail Farm*, and my niece Nikki's *Lady's Hat Farm*'s homemade Red Fife Sourdough bread and coleslaw. It was truly a feast for all senses: so colourful, wholesome, and healthy. I filled my plate with the delicious offerings and ate every bite! Given that I was not much more than skin and bones at that point, everyone was pleasantly shocked at the amount I consumed! I later learned that the dexamethasone that I'd been taking since the day I was medivaced down to Edmonton is also known to stimulate appetite.

There were more tears, strong hugs, and promises to never forget how much I was loved as we loaded up the vehicles and hit the country highways back to the big city. We decided that Mom and Kirst would drive back together so that Lisa and I could share a few more hours together before we said our "so long for now". Plus, it also gave Dr. Lisa Yang an opportunity to have a professional discussion with my husband so that he could better understand the importance of ensuring my needs were honoured. She delivered the important message of the fact that his wife had cancer and was thus at a far greater risk of developing blood clots far more gently yet firmly than I could. Thus my needing a break to stretch my legs was not just me being demanding. It made me wish we lived closer to one another, so that she could be our family physician.

I attempted to alleviate Robert's stress by ensuring I was in physical contact with him, holding his hand or with my arm around his shoulder the majority of the drive back to the loft.

Papa Bear arrives!

Kirst and Mom picked Dad up at the airport and brought him directly to the loft after his delayed flights from New Brunswick. I'm proud to say that our dad gives the most exuberant, rib-cracking, warm hugs a person could ever ask for—truly. And given his relief to finally be in the same air space as me, my twin sis, and our mom. Another characteristic of our dad is that he's a talker; plus, he's hard of hearing and isn't entirely convinced he requires a hearing aid notwithstanding our insistence to the contrary. Despite Mom having given him the heads up about my being very easily over-stimulated sensorially, he didn't absorb the message for several days, which made our initial time together a huge adjustment. It was tough, because we didn't wish to hurt his feelings, but I just could not take the constant yet seemingly anxious attempts at conversation: particularly because he has the tendency to pick a topic (often relating to politics) and repeatedly express the same opinions. I adore my dad, but I got blunt with him more than once in those first few days, telling him that he wasn't to talk about that topic if it was something ultimately upsetting to me. Mom worked on him too, as there were several taboo topics. As the days grew into weeks, the adjustment grew easier.

Another gift we received from Robert's long-time friends, Jeff and Joanne, was the opportunity for us to housesit at their acreage in Spruce Grove and dog sit their precious pooch, Moose. On the first night, Robert's mom, Anne, and her husband visited. As soon as she saw me, Anne had tears and pulled me into a hug like I've never received from her in the previous twenty years of our relationship. I was moved to tears too. She appeared older, and quite visibly shaken. I felt so much love for and from her. The next morning, Anne presented me with a gorgeous scarf that I wore daily. Once I began to lose my hair, I also wore it wrapped like a turban atop my balding skull.

I had another channelling session with Jillian. I was grateful for the privacy of the master suite, while Mom and Dad were upstairs in their guest suite, as there were many tears shed through the healing process. It was reaffirmed that I was on my way to healing, but there still remained a great deal of work to do in terms of peeling back these next layers of self-forgiveness, self-grief, etc. When Jillian followed up after asking how I was feeling, I responded, "Brilliant!" She continued to send me love as I worked through this powerful process, and towards the end of the month, I was sleeping a lot more.

I took great pleasure at being the person to feed, water, walk, and administer meds to Moose, who was nursing an injury to a tendon in his knee, sustained when he attempted to chase a moose. He fed my need for four-legged companionship, as it was hard being away from our two dogs back in Yellowknife, especially given that Scooby was so ill.

While we were at the Granbergs', another Yellowknife friend, former student and registered massage therapist, Cailey, made a trip to Spruce Grove to visit and gift me a lymphatic foot and face massage on Sunday. We spent the first hour visiting over coffee and tea before she and I went into the master suite and she pampered me for another hour. I was a total space cadet by the end—so relaxed and blissed out! Later that evening, I was contacted by another Yellowknife friend and fellow yoga instructor, Christa, who was hosting a "108 Wishes for Maureen" meditation event at Collective Soul Space. This was a prearranged conversation. There were over twenty in attendance, and I chatted and answered all of their questions for me for about fifteen minutes before they rang off to begin their chanting of the 108 Wishes within the Sivananda tradition. I rested on the bed as I wished to fully absorb the beautiful energy of the wishes that they were sending my way.

As the Spring Equinox approached, my sleeping patterns only got more sporadic, especially as there was a full moon around the same time. I was getting up to meditate in the early morning hours, often going out to the living room and turning on the gigantic Himalayan salt lamp to serve as a light source.

When we arrived at the CCI, we learned that my radiation/chemo protocol would be six weeks in length, starting the following day. We went back to the acreage soon after that appointment to get laundry done and get packed to move back to the loft.

Also on our last day at the acreage, I received a message from Cailey's mom, Susan. Would I be interested in two tickets to see Michelle Obama? *Would I?* Obviously, generosity runs in that family! Overwhelmed by her gesture but also at the prospect of beginning my treatments, believe it or not, I didn't immediately accept, letting her know that I was going to be starting my six-week radiation/chemo protocol the following day and was unsure of the effect it would have on me. I expressed my gratitude for her offer but asked if she could give me a couple of days to let her know. Fortunately, with the ability to send and receive tickets online, she took no issue with my request.

Robert and I had a group radiation meeting, during which time I recall Robert having as close to a panic attack as I think I've ever seen him have. He hadn't realized that the meeting was only about educating about the radiation and the chemo education was separate. It was all smoothed out over tea in the CCI cafe before we made our way to the pharmacy to get our chemo talk with Roland. We had time to drop off many of our belongings to the loft before making our way back to Spruce Grove to say a sad goodbye to Moose and our temporary luxury lodgings, and gather Mom and Dad and move them into their loft.

Mike and April, my radiation techs, teased me about my Pippi Longstocking hairstyle once locked into the mask, as he had to tie up my then full, luscious auburn locks into pigtails for the treatment. They learned quickly that playing music of any kind during my ten-to-fifteen-minute sessions was a no-no, as I wished to use the time to meditate.

My chemo protocol required me to take my antibiotic two hours before my radiation treatment and my antiemetic one hour before. I began the following day, and fortunately, didn't feel much of anything in the way of side effects. My dosage for chemo over the six weeks was 125 mg of Temozolomide—TMZ—a drug shown to be quite effective for my type of brain tumour. It is in pill-form, which seems atypical, and is only used in two forms of cancer, with GBM being the primary one.

A Chance of a Lifetime

In conversation with Mike and April, I let them know of my friend's invitation to give me tickets to see Michelle Obama and my worry that I'd not be able to enjoy her talk due to side effects. Mike reassured me that because I was in the first week of my protocol, chances were solid that I would be fine. I contacted Susan and we arranged for her to email me the tickets. Now, who to bring with me?

Before I could get that question answered, Kirst called with a shakily urgent request to speak with me. I asked her what was up, and she said, "I just met Michelle Obama!" I had forgotten that was happening that night, when Kirst burst into tears and said, "You're going to meet her tomorrow night!" I was stunned, and then started crying myself. Kirst went on to explain that during the "Meet and Greet", Mrs. Obama warmly hugged her and when asked if she could get an extra long hug, the answer was, "Of course; what's goin' on, girl?" While still hugging, Kirst told her that her identical twin was just diagnosed with terminal brain cancer. When Kirst shared that I was receiving treatment in Edmonton, the former First Lady said, "Edmonton! We are there tomorrow night!" After Kirsten explained that I had a ticket to attend, but not to the "Meet and Greet", Mrs. Obama's response was, "I can do better than that." Mrs. Obama called out to her trusted Chief of Staff of many years, Melissa, introducing her to Kirsten saying, "This favour's on me!" Unreal! A flurry of emails went back and forth between Melissa and myself, as arrangements were made.

Given the quality of the seats, I figured my sis-in-law Kathy would be most game and available to come to town early, as we were going to be shown first-class treatment, with a personal concierge to boot. Kathy was thrilled to have gotten the invitation, though she was teased by her family that the one sister who initially had relatively little interest by comparison, would in fact be invited to meet Michelle Obama in person!

Earlier that day, I'd made an emergency phone call to the Radiation Department to see if it would be at all possible to come in earlier for my radiation appointment explaining my reasoning. Very graciously, they agreed to have me come in around midday. I excitedly explained to the radiation techs on duty what was happening for me later that day—they shared in my excitement and asked to hear all about my experience.

As we made our way upstairs to the Gretzky-themed Studio 99 in Rogers Place, our concierge took our coats and handbags, as we would not be allowed to take them into the cordoned and curtained area where the meet and greet was taking place. We were selected to be the final guests to meet Michelle Obama, with the Secret Service standing immediately behind us.

As we inched our way closer into the curtained area, we could see Mrs. Obama: she is even more stunningly statuesque and genuine in person! I had a hard time taking my eyes off her. But I did notice someone looking at me. With a huge smile and an enthusiastic wave, Melissa called out to me: "You must be Kirsten's twin!" We laughed and later hugged, as Kathy and I were suddenly the next ones to meet the former First Lady. She stood facing us, with her arms wide open. I began to cry and was tongue-tied as I attempted to explain who I was. We hugged and I thanked her profusely for the gift of the meet and greet tickets. She said that it was her pleasure, and then asked to be introduced to Kathy. We had the requisite photo op before Kathy and I were escorted out. My legs were heavy from the energy expenditure, and I needed to sit down once in the main arena while Kathy got more water for us.

In the arena, there was a highly entertaining montage of video clips of Michelle over the years: on daytime and nighttime talk shows, on *Sesame Street*, and more. I did find the sound to be overwhelmingly loud, fervently wishing I had brought earplugs with me. Within twenty minutes of finding our seats, the show began. It was enthralling, with *Good Morning America*'s Robin Roberts moderating this "intimate conversation" in front of thousands! I hadn't yet read the former FLOTUS's book: *Becoming,* but after being thoroughly wrapped up in her stories I knew I would.

As fascinated as I was with the opportunity to see Michelle Obama live, I maxed out in terms of my sensory tolerance towards the end. We elected to beat the crowds, leaving about ten minutes before the actual end. Kathy spent the night on the sofa in our loft and departed early the following morning after expressing her profound gratitude for evening.

My bestie Natalie had arrived the night before, and we shared a love-filled weekend, spending time at the local Good Earth Coffeehouse and having a much-needed heart-to-heart about what had actually been going on since January. We were both in tears at times, as she described how she really hadn't been doing at all well with the news. But Kirst had shared my actual prognosis with Nat, so her struggle was entirely understandable. In seeing me in person—how much better I was doing just since January—Nat felt considerably relieved, though still not 100% convinced that I was going to embody my adopted hashtags: #MightyMo and #cancerthriver.

Later on Saturday, I treated Nat to a pedicure. I had decided to go with four different colours: each one featured in my "Radiance M-bodied Yoga" logo, my business moniker. I loved showing off my toes! Nat departed on the Sunday afternoon, and we tearily hugged the stuffing out of one another, openly expressing our mutual adoration and honouring her "honorary fifth Tonge daughter" status.

We appreciated all of the visitors we had during this time.

For friends and family who weren't able to visit in person, there was another opportunity to make a significant difference: through the GoFundMe account set up by a childhood friend, Christine. Spending many a weekend bowling, camping, and enjoying sleepovers at her dad and stepmom's place in our hometown of Quispamsis, NB, Kirsten, Christine, and I shared a close connection despite now being on the opposite sides of the country. Christine had set up this account, after suggesting it a few weeks earlier to Kirsten. Her touching and ardent plea for financial support in order that my immediate family would have one less thing to worry about was enthusiastically received. In a very short period of time, over $14,000 was raised, all of which, minus administrative fees, has been used to bring my parents and Tonge daughters together more than once in 2019. It was staggering to the family how much support we received, literally from all corners of the globe.

Chapter 8

Transitions

AS WE NEARED the end of March, we also neared the end of Robert's available time to remain with me in Edmonton, as he had obtained new employment at one of Canada's diamond mines, Rio Tinto's Diavik Diamond Mine. Fortunately, his new boss was extremely compassionate in allowing Robert to defer his start date to April 1st, 2019. In the last few days of our time together, he ensured all of my ducks were in a row, so that I would have no issues whatsoever. He was far more nervous about leaving me than I was. I was excited for him to have the opportunity to think about something else besides the health of his wife! I knew that he would be amply challenged returning to the type of work that would stimulate his brilliant planning brain after a year and a half away from that field of his expertise.

Before he left, Robert escorted me to attend my second Healing Sound Bath and it was there that I was introduced to Bev Ross, a certified vibroacoustic harp therapist (VAHT). I'd been entirely enraptured by the sound of the harp throughout the lunchtime healing sound bath and introduced myself following the session. We sat and chatted pleasantly about my experience, specifically about what was going on with me, and to my utter delight, she invited me to experience the gift of a private VAHT session with her at her home at my convenience!

Kathy arrived as Robert headed to the airport to fly home. She showed up bearing a treasure trove of homemade goodness. It was her pleasure to bring dinner: a from-scratch, made with much love Indian dish named Keema. She had only just returned from a month-long retreat to Kerala, India early in March. Kathy also brought a freezer full of homemade bone broth, as well as more meat from her son's RedTail Farm.

We spent a chunk of that day running errands as we would no longer have access to a vehicle until Robert returned on Good Friday. On Sunday, we visited the Art Gallery of Alberta and thoroughly appreciated learning more about Indigenous trauma and efforts of healing with Reconciliation.

Mom, Dad, and I relished our time with Kathy and were sad to say goodbye on Monday morning. I felt even more connected to her after that special weekend, as she and I had some important and deep spiritual conversations.

Nervous System Dis-regulation and Healing Trauma

I had naively believed in March that I would have the time and energy to complete a thirteen-week online course called "Smart Body, Smart Mind™", by Irene Lyon. I was "in" for sure. Irene has a vast, encyclopaedic knowledge of the nervous system and how trauma impacts it and our ability to heal.

I signed up for this course. I did well to complete the first few labs, which involved watching videos and participating in live Facebook chats and training calls as well as guided practices and homework. However, I underestimated how much of a time commitment it would be, and fell behind rather rapidly, especially with the number of guests and family members visiting us at the loft. It proved to be a solid lesson in boundary setting, and to not be so hard on myself for sure.

It was Mom and Dad who walked with me each day to my daily appointments. I loved having my parents to myself. Mom and Dad enjoyed meeting the "regulars" that were on a similar schedule as me for radiation. I connected closely with an elderly couple.

One of them got to ring the Bell of Hope before me, and we showed up early that day just so that we could witness him ring it. I brought a bouquet of tulips and we said a tearful goodbye.

Following Kirst's return the night before, on Saturday, the four of us ventured to the weekly Old Strathcona Farmers' Market, electing to walk rather than taking a cab or an Uber. It was still feeling like late winter, but the fresh air was magnificent. It was good to get a bit of a workout.

The following day dawned sunny and bright, so we took an Uber to one of the parks by the North Saskatchewan River which runs through the middle of the city. We had fun going up and then down the Funicular by the Fairmont Hotel Macdonald, after I admitted needing to use the facilities. After, we managed to find a bus to take us within a few short blocks to the loft. We had to run to catch it, which I'm sure was rather entertaining to watch! My legs were ridiculously weak, and I felt entirely uncoordinated trying to lift them to run. It was a very bizarre and uncomfortable sensation to be sure: definitely what I'd come to refer to as my "chemo legs". I was impressed with the speed at which our senior parents moved!

Debbie had flown in from Yellowknife to stay with me for a week. We spent a good deal of time walking, window shopping, and drinking coconut milk mochas or lattes at the Good Earth Coffeehouse. She was blown away by my energy levels. Prior to arriving, she'd anticipated that she'd get a lot of reading done because I'd be spending much of my time in bed! Not so. I went to my first of several VAHT sessions with my new friend, Bev Ross.

How it worked is that I lay down on a bed with a special pad on it containing two speakers. Her harp was connected to the speakers. She spent the first few minutes playing seven series of chords, with my identifying which one(s) I felt most appealing within each of the series. Then Bev began to play, based on which notes I had identified. I did my best to stay conscious, but at some point, I dozed off—into a deep restorative sleep that involved gentle snoring, apparently! As Bev was wrapping up, I came to, feeling quite moved and very relaxed on all levels.

That afternoon, I got a note from Susan, the friend who had gifted me the tickets to Michelle Obama. "What does your Monday night look like? I have four tickets to Michael Bublé if you can make it." Omigosh! I love Michael Bublé! I didn't hesitate to accept, as I knew Mom and Dad would also love to attend. We couldn't wait for Monday night to arrive!

Special Moments and Special Memories Are Made

It was back to the business of bloodwork, chemo, and radiation the following day, but the end was in sight. Before that happened, however, there was so much fun to be had! What with our Michael Bublé concert happening that night, my youngest sister, Melanie's long-awaited visit, and Mom and Dad's fifty-fourth wedding anniversary, there was no chance of being bored. On Good Friday, Robert was returning for the long Easter weekend.

In the last two and a half weeks of my concurrent radiation/chemo protocol, I finally got my ideal timeslot: 11:00 am. This time allowed me to comfortably take my meds prior to breakfast and still feel like I had the whole day ahead of me once I was done with my radiation. One thing that had changed was that I no longer had to take the antibiotic that had been prescribed, as the additional blood work I had indicated an allergy to Dapsone. I quite enjoyed taking one fewer pill a day, frankly, which is funny for me to say considering the crazy number of supplements I now take. But I feel far better taking supplements than I do a harsh antibiotic that I truly didn't require in the first place.

Not only did Michael Bublé blow our socks off with his witty repartee, but his vast musical talent and the talents of his orchestra were indescribably impressive! The lights, digital effects, and volume were at times overstimulating for my poor brain, to be sure; but I was still blown away by the show, as were Mom and Dad.

I loved how human Michael Bublé was: talking about his young son Noah's illness at three years old: his eventual recovery from liver cancer and the impact it had on his family. He allowed the emotions to come up, and I felt such a strong connection with him at that time. He shared the same beliefs as I and many others, to be sure, about the importance of believing in the body's ability to heal; the importance of a gratitude practice, and always coming from a place of love. I found myself in tears more than once.

Mom and Dad celebrated their fifty-fourth wedding anniversary with family at Earls. For Mel, it had been a very long and anxiety-filled six weeks of waiting to visit.

The following evening, my friend Andrea, and a former student of both of ours, Angie, showed up to cut my hair. We had decided earlier to make a Facebook Live video of this process, and invited folks to participate in the call. We got me set up on a stool in the kitchen, and got down to business. It was an absolute blast! Andrea videoed and shared the comments that folks were making, to which I responded with greetings and often telling stories about the people who were commenting. There was so much laughter, and so many people participating, that it was an unforgettable experience for me. And from the response I received, people thoroughly enjoyed my stories and the opportunity to vicariously experience my new look.

Good Friday was indeed so good! Robert returned and was at the loft by 9:00 am and we were on the road with Mom, Dad, and Mel. It was a bit of a tight squeeze to get everybody in for the drive to Castor, given there was also luggage as we'd be there for two nights, but the drive was entertaining and scenic.

We arrived in Castor and went immediately to Anne and Bill's to have lunch with whomever could make it. Kathy was away, but prior to her departure, she'd offered her lovely "Grouse House" for Robert and I to stay in so that we'd have privacy and a getaway for me when things got too loud. We could not have asked for a more peaceful place to stay those two nights in Castor.

Mealtimes are always entertaining with the Castor Clan, and once my brother-in-law and his family arrived, it got even more so! Melanie has a wickedly witty sense of humour, and though it was her first time in ten years (since I got married) seeing them, she didn't hold back. We were all in stitches! We dined potluck style. In keeping with the Catholic tradition of fish on Fridays, Anne cooked up a couple of huge salmon filets. I adore Robert's boisterous family. I loved that they non-judgmentally respected my need to remove myself when things got too loud. I also loved how they welcomed my family as part of their own.

I find myself particularly impacted by the cycles of the moon, and with the full moon my sleep was interrupted. As a light sleeper, my husband woke up with my restlessness. I got up and went outside to take pictures of the full moon and its reflection on the snowy field. But the air was also breathtaking, literally, so I went back indoors and crawled back into bed. We dozed off and on until about 6:30 am. Holding onto one another tightly, and feeling incredibly in love, I blurted out a thought that had occurred to me in my dreams: "Hey hon; wanna renew our wedding vows in honour of our tenth wedding anniversary this summer?" Robert said, "YES!" I began to laugh. I was immediately taken back to the memory of when I proposed to him ten years before, except that his response wasn't the enthusiastic affirmation as he'd come up with this time. You see, ten years ago, I had put the question(s) to him this way: "Do you realize that our two families have never been all together in the ten years that we've been together? I'd like to celebrate our ten-year anniversary of being together by throwing an 'East Coast Kitchen Party'-type celebration and actually get married. What do you think? Would you like to get married?" His response triggered my, "I'm never enough" response, when he replied, "Let me think about it and get back to you." Seriously!? I was really hurt! That said, he came around to the idea within a couple of days, and then had a great time taking charge of the music he wanted—keeping it a surprise for me, and even arranging for a live band consisting of a bunch of his buddies that he'd grown up with in Hudson Bay, SK. They were a highlight of our East Coast Kitchen Party wedding and were talked about for months afterwards.

Easter Sunday dawned sunny and relatively mild, and a few of us went out for some fresh air and exercise. When we came upon a hopscotch game painted on the park pavement, I decided to test my endurance and my balance; I didn't do too badly at all! Mel videotaped it and I later posted it as an Instagram update. It felt really good to tap into some childlike behaviour, throwing caution to the wind and just going for it! I was pretty pooped, though, by the time we got back to Anne and Bill's.

The rest of the day flew by and before we knew it, it was time to bid farewell to the Castor Clan and hit the road back to Edmonton and get Mel to the airport. We were all tired but entirely content with our time together with everyone, and soon we were able to crawl tiredly into our beds in our respective lofts.

Robert was able to accompany me to my radiation appointment on Monday and drop me off for my next VAHT session with Bev prior to continuing on to the airport. We wouldn't see one another until the following Sunday morning, when he returned to witness me wrap up my six-week concurrent radiation/chemo protocol and finally ring the Bell of Hope!

With Robert gone, Nat accompanied me to my treatments. Plus, she, Mom, and Dad joined me for the monthly Healing Sound Bath. They loved it! I again spoke with the musician, Sparrow, afterwards summarizing my appreciation of the three Healing Sound Baths I'd experienced, asking her if she'd mind singing the song again that had resulted in my tears during the first sound bath. She graciously played the entire song, not just the chorus, explaining that it was originally the Judds' song and that I'd be able to find it on Spotify.

Later that evening, all four of us headed to the airport, as it was time to bid adieu to my parents until the end of June, when they would be returning to Yellowknife along with my siblings for a week. There were tears, but also a great deal of laughter and a massive amount of unabashed love expressed by all. Mom and Dad were able to get on the plane knowing that I would continue to thrive as the weeks progressed.

The following day, Nat's last day with me until late May, I treated her to a float at Edmonton Float House. Yes, I was braving it again after my disastrous experience at the Float House in Abbotsford. It was totally worth it. We both were able to fully relax and enjoy our time in our cabins and emerged quite Zen, deciding not to rush out but rather to enjoy a cup of tea, after which Nat returned home.

Kirst arrived overnight, electing to stay in a hotel due to her late night arrival. She showed up in time to escort me to my radiation appointment at CCI.

As the end of the month drew nearer, I was thrilled to welcome Robert back so that he could be with me to share in the auspicious occasions of my final two radiation treatments and ringing the Bell of Hope on April 30th. When the three of us arrived at Unit 9 Radiation waiting area, we were thrilled to see that the friends we had made were also there, with a bouquet of flowers and a card for me! Their son had driven them in specially to witness me ring the bell. When it was my time to go in for my very last radiation session, I was giddy with joy.

Within twenty minutes, I emerged dancing, and then rang the Bell of Hope three times, which Kirsten videoed on her phone while simultaneously taking pictures with my phone—entirely impressive! I first hugged and kissed my husband, then Kirst, then hugged pretty much everyone in Unit 9 that I'd had the pleasure of being a "regular" with and getting to know, which included at least a half-dozen of the radiation techs!

Ringing the Bell of Hope
April 30, 2019

My bubble was burst when we met with the licenced Nurse Practitioner (LPN) in charge of my file. When he came into the office, he asked me how I was feeling to which I replied that I felt fantastic. His response pissed me off, and I didn't make much of an attempt to hide my facial reaction; if he'd been looking at me instead of at his computer screen, he might have seen my incredulous look. He said: "That's fine that you're feeling good now, but it won't last." Huh?! In my mind, I had a hissy fit: *Who are you to tell me how I'll feel? You don't know me!* I chose to stay silent, with some difficulty. I was determined to live my life in a more positive and healthier mindset as it had been serving me well to this point and quite frankly, it's the way I operate the vast majority of the time!

Chapter 9

Spring into Summer

A Week of Respite

KIRSTEN WAS LEAVING the next day to fly home to Abbotsford, so I walked her to where she was staying with friends, visited for a bit, and said our "Ciao for Niao"s, knowing we'd see one another again in three and a half weeks as we were going to be spending our birthday together for the first time since 2016. Robert and I began to pack up that evening finishing last-minute details and scouring our loft the next morning as there was an inspection planned before we checked out at noon. At this time, I was particularly happy for my hubby's attention to detail and his tendency to work fast and efficiently, even though I felt some pressure to try to keep up. The check-out procedure went smoothly, and we were soon on the road to take the Granbergs up on their generous offer to spend a night at their condo in Canmore before we headed to Banff for two nights. Happy to get out of the city, we thoroughly enjoyed the over-three-hour drive on rural roads into the foothills. Once we reached the condo, we gloried in its peaceful and quiet atmosphere. I took pleasure in creating a sustaining healthy dinner for us and we had an early night after such a full day.

I could have easily stayed in Canmore for a few more days; however, as a celebratory gesture for having completed my six-week protocol of radiation and chemo, my husband treated me to two nights at the Fairmont Banff Springs; a deluxe historic landmark hotel in the Châteauesque architectural style. I was spoiled, as our room had an incredible mountain valley view. He had booked us on to the exclusive fifth floor, which meant we had access to a private lounge with a free buffet of Happy Hour appetizers, non-alcoholic beverages, and breakfast included for the two nights we were there. Alcoholic beverages could be purchased, but I'd given up alcohol early in the New Year.

I'd not experienced anything so luxurious before in my life. For our first night there, dear friends of ours, Larry and Diane Lozinski drove almost two hours from Calgary just to treat us to dinner and get a much-anticipated visit in.

We also shared with them our intention to renew our vows that July and I rather precociously invited them to Yellowknife to join us, as they'd been at our wedding ten years prior. Robert was quick to let them know it wasn't necessary, but they enthusiastically responded that they'd love to.

When we returned to our room, I learned from our dog-sitting neighbours that our dog, Scooby, had stopped eating and taking water and had lost the ability to walk, and had lost control of his bowels. We called them, and with us all on speaker phone, Denise put the phone to Scoob's ear, and I spoke directly with him, telling him to hold on, that his mama was going to be home soon. I told him how I just knew that he would wait for our return. Ray and Denise agreed to deliver Scoob to our place within a half hour prior to our return on Sunday.

The following morning, after the fresh air and exercise we had and the emotional upset of the night before, I had the need to nap in the afternoon. Robert and I then spent additional time reading and relaxing in the fifth-floor lounge taking advantage of the Happy Hour spread, but not overindulging as we had made reservations for our last night in Banff at another of the hotel's restaurants: the Waldhaus.

We checked out the following morning, loaded up the truck, and began our backcountry highway drive to Gull Lake, where we'd spend our final night of what I've coined as my Respite Time at our friends' the Granberg's cottage on Gull Lake. We drove roads that even Robert had not yet driven, despite having spent about a decade of his tween and teen years in Alberta. It was beautiful, and I lost count of the wildlife, horses, and cattle we saw through the foothills.

Once there, we were welcomed with open arms—and I expressed our profound gratitude to them in person. Their "cottage" is way more than that, and the four of us thoroughly enjoyed our short time together, as they were leaving the next morning to catch a plane to Madrid. We left later in the day to make our way to Leduc to drop off Bill's truck at our niece's acreage and she would then take us to the airport. We were soon on our way home.

Yellowknife Bound!

We arrived home late in the evening on Sunday, but given the lengthening days, it was still light enough to view from my window seat the immense vastness of Great Slave Lake. We approached the rocky outcrops, smaller lakes, and curious combination of buildings that comprise the capital city of Yellowknife—home! I was teary as we descended: emotional not only because I was finally home, but also because I knew I'd be saying goodbye to my best four-legged friend for the past fourteen years.

Other friends were willing to keep our dog Tillie with them one more night so that Robert and I could be alone with Scoob. With my heart in my throat, we quietly entered so as not to disturb our wee boy. He didn't even stir. I was crying and speaking to him, "Scooby, your mama's home, baby boy. Oh my wee boy, I love you so much." He opened his eyes, clouded with cataracts, and his tiny stub of a tail wagged as he recognized that we were home. I did my best to avoid sobbing, as I'd been informed that it adds stress to the dog when they see you crying.

I soon noticed that he'd soiled himself as his organs were shutting down. I gently bathed his bum, and had Robert assist me in putting clean towels down on the dog bed as I held his weak body. I was so grateful that he had hung on until I got home.

I set up a bed for myself beside him. I spent his last two days beside him constantly, except to take Tillie out as required. I would pour water in my hand or wet my fingers so that he could lick what he could. I would carry him outside to see if he would do his business—he was wobbly at best and couldn't walk so I gently held him up around his ribcage. After a discussion with Robert, I called the vet on Monday. The Yellowknife Veterinary Clinic staff were incredibly kind over the phone. Tillie kept her distance, rarely venturing close, except for a couple of times when she wanted to lie by the patio door, which was where Scoob's bed was. She obviously sensed something was up. We didn't force her to get close, and Scoob was oblivious to her presence and rarely awake.

We got the call. It was a team effort to move him to Robert's truck. We laid him in the back seat, and I climbed in. He was awake but transitioning. I spoke to him throughout the ride. We were directed to a room, and Dr. Hughes came in to tell us how things would happen. He then left to give us time to say our goodbyes. Upon his return, he told us that once the needle was inserted, death would come quickly and painlessly. I had been playing different versions of the traditional Kundalini chant for acknowledging and honouring the soul after it leaves the physical body, chanting along with the music. Robert left the room to take care of payment and to give me more time alone with Scoob's cooling body. I held him close and chanted "Akaal" (deathless) at the top of my voice for several minutes until Robert and Dr. Hughes returned. Dr. Hughes picked Scoob up and carried him to the back room, where his body would be sent south to Edmonton for cremation. In addition to a small box that contained our wee boy's ashes, the clinic also gifted us a handmade wooden box that had room for a photo in the cover, and inside was a plaster cast of Scooby's paw with his name stamped on it.

Once back in the truck, I wailed. When we got home, a bemused Tillie was curled up in her bed. I wrapped myself around her and let her know that her "little big brother" had crossed the Rainbow Bridge. She continues to grieve his loss, but in her own way.

I had another session with Jillian two days later. I had to forgive myself for not being there physically for Scoob in his last two months. I felt dramatically lighter in my heart afterwards. It was a necessary time of healing, and I have to say that as a direct result of this session, my active grieving time has been dramatically shortened.

I was easily exhausted in those early days, so I needed to ensure I napped most afternoons. But I did find some time to spend with friends. On Thursday, I had a phone appointment with an ND from NamasteMD: a company that provides legal medical cannabis and CBD in whatever format is the preference of the person applying. I'd decided to integrate this modality into my routine after reading an article in *Maclean's* magazine. I was approved for six months of a combination of CBD and THC oil.

My first appointment with my family doc took place the next day. She was supportive of my journey, and ensured I had what I needed in terms of a monthly requisition for blood work, as I would be commencing my first of six rounds of chemo in early June. She too was impressed to see how well-functioning I was, not that she'd seen me at my worst, but she had read the report sent up by CCI. That week, I'd begun titrating off my dexamethasone from two pills to one a day, which I was quite happy to be doing. Being on it had helped save my life by reducing the edema in my brain for which I was grateful, but it had caused what's called "moon face" and belly bloat: common side effects of this drug. Also common is increased appetite, which I didn't mind and increased hair growth, which I'd been noticing particularly on my face; the hair was soft and fuzzy. I used my husband's razor to shave it a couple of times when it felt like I was growing a beard and moustache! Thankfully, once I titrated completely off of the dexamethasone, all of the side effects I'd experienced stopped.

Saturday of the May long weekend was a gorgeous sunny day, and I headed out for a drive with Tillie along the Ingraham Trail: a seventy km chip seal and gravel road to "nowhere" as it ends abruptly at Tibbett Lake three seasons of the year. That morning, Tillie and I were going to visit my friend and fellow Collective Soul Space member, Johanna Tiemessen, who lives off-grid at Prelude East. I let Jo know how my Full Flower Moon Meditation and Healing Gong Bath Fundraiser for the Brain Tumour Foundation of Canada had gone the night before— highly successfully with over thirty in attendance! In the summer, I felt that all I could healthily commit to was a once-monthly Full Moon Meditation and Gong Bath in July and August.

A chunk of the rest of the long weekend was spent completing the paperwork to apply for long term disability with Yellowknife Education District #1 and my insurance company. It was tedious, but necessary, in order to be able to facilitate the payment of all of the expensive integrative treatments that I would be pursuing. I dropped off the paperwork to District Office two days prior to my departure to Vancouver. I was grateful for Robert's assistance in ensuring I'd completed everything as required. By the time I arrived in Vancouver, I was tuckered out.

On the Road Again

Kirst had arranged for us to join a buddy of hers to drive us to Chilliwack to see a high school friend—now a professional blues musician based out of Montreal—perform. Though I was exhausted, I tagged along, as it had been close to thirty years since I'd seen him and had never seen him perform. I am glad I went as it was truly wonderful to see Rob perform—such bluesy talent. The evening took a lot out of me and I slept much of the drive back to Kirst's townhouse. We had a quiet Friday, thankfully, which allowed me to recoup my energy. My exhaustion also prompted Kirsten to realize that we needed to find accommodation in Vancouver for our birthday, May 25th, after attending a very special concert that was a bucket list item for me. While still in Edmonton, I'd purchased three tickets to see Bhakti Yogis: Deva Premal, Miten, and Manose perform at UBC's Chan Centre for the Performing Arts. Though Kirst was only familiar with the one song for which Deva Premal is best known ("Gayatri Mantra"), she was glad to tag along. The third ticket I gave to a dear friend, Yolaine.

Prior to our heading back into Vancouver for the concert, Kirst had really wanted to stop by Devan Greenhouses to stock up on the flowers she wished to plant on her balcony and wished for my input. I was happy to go, seeing as I love planting flowers and it would be at least two weeks before it would be warm enough in Yellowknife for me to plant. The greenhouses there were huge, and I'll admit to feeling envious that there was a far greater variety of flowers and greenery available there that I'd have access to. Ah, the joys of living so far away in Canada's subarctic! While wandering up and down the aisles of the greenhouse, we spotted a very familiar figure: Dad's youngest brother, our Uncle Frank! He was thrilled to see us, and waved to our Aunt Bonnie. They hadn't seen me since before I'd gotten sick and had been understandably concerned. We hugged and gabbed. It was an unexpected joy to have run into them. Kirst and I soon made our way to the checkout as we had spent longer than anticipated and needed to get the plants to her place and hit the road to Vancouver.

Kirst had arranged for us to stay in one of the student residences at University of British Columbia as an economical option that was easy walking distance to the Chan Centre. She and I had checked into the residence and had a chance to relax before meeting up with Yolaine. Yo was already at the restaurant with birthday gifts for each of us, and another long-time friend, Katherine Wright joined us soon after we arrived. Each gift was thoughtfully selected. I have worn the gorgeous colourful scarf she'd purchased for me on a recent trip to Ireland just about every day this past winter! She also treated Kirst and I to dinner prior to the concert. All three of us piled into Kirst's car after saying our goodbyes to Katherine, to drive to the Chan Centre.

The concert was all that I'd hoped it would be! Truly a dream come true. I chanted and danced along with hundreds of others in the audience. Yo and Kirst got a big kick out of my enthusiasm, which I think they found infectious as none of us could stop smiling. There was an intermission and we headed outside to get some fresh air and catch a lovely pink sunset that we could view through the trees. I was enjoying not having to wear too many layers! It was an utter joy to see them perform many traditional Sanskrit chants live. Audience participation was encouraged, as they projected the lyrics of the chants on a huge screen above and behind them, which I belted out enthusiastically. After the concert, Kirst and I walked Yo to the bus stop and made our way to our room where we both fell almost instantly asleep.

It was a stunningly beautiful morning, so we drove to Jericho Beach in Lower Point Grey/Kitsilano prior to driving back to Abbotsford. Though sunny, it wasn't warm which didn't stop us from removing our shoes and socks to walk along the water's edge and even venturing knee deep into the water a couple of times! Both Kirst and I are incredibly connected to the element of water, feeling at home "in, on, or under" it. Perhaps it was a result of being raised on the East Coast, and all of the times we would go to various beaches on the Bay of Fundy, I don't know. Being on the West Coast, the Pacific Ocean feels energetically different but simultaneously so good. After walking for a while, we sat and revelled in the view, enjoying people- and dog-watching.

Monday, we had made plans to go to Coquitlam to have dinner with our cousin, Reese and his partner, Janet. We loved our too-brief visit and it was wonderful to be able to talk openly about some of the "woo woo" experiences I'd been having in recent months. We spent the entire visit outdoors under their lanai, enjoying the sun under protective covering.

On Tuesday morning, Kirst drove us to Fort Langley, situated at the northern tip of the township of Langley on the shores of the Fraser River. It also featured a renowned Integrated Clinic with a specialized Cancer Centre. Kirst had been instrumental in getting me set up with an appointment for that morning with Naturopathic Doctor Erik Boudreau, who is a specialist in brain cancer. Dr. Boudreau was an amazing listener. It was an hour-long appointment that included a recommended protocol to follow regarding integrative treatments such as IV Immunotherapies, Hyperthermia, and Helixor A (Mistletoe Therapy). What I truly appreciated was Dr. Boudreau's communication style: friendly, open, and genuinely interested. Given that I live far away, he was quick to mention that I'd be welcome to do any or all of my treatments in Yellowknife or Edmonton, as he recognized the reality of my not being able to commit to being in B.C. for six straight weeks to complete them. He was pleasantly surprised that I had already been taking twenty mg of melatonin since my diagnosis and was quick to compliment me on all that I had been doing to date.

Specifically, he referenced my positive attitude, my recognition of the connection between mind, body, and spirit, as well as the importance of nutrition in combating cancer. He mentioned that I might want to consider adopting the ketogenic diet at some point, as studies had shown it to be particularly effective, especially in brain cancer cases. He also had some supplement recommendations such as Can-Arrest by Vitazan Professionals, ECGC (otherwise known as Green Tea Extract), vitamin E and vitamin A and more. He was fine with my taking all of the other supplements in the Lifestyle Vitality, and the use of essential oils. We met briefly with the manager of the Cancer Centre where he printed out and presented us with the price breakdown of all of the treatments. I will admit to experiencing "sticker shock" as the price was around $10,000, none of which would be covered by insurance. They didn't expect me to commit to anything that day except to pay for my one-hour consultation.

Cowtown

A mutual friend of ours happened to work at YYC, so he offered to take me to Nat's.

Nat has two daughters who are incredibly strong in personality and I like to think will help change the world. Nat's teen daughter, in particular, seems to feel that I'm a bit of a kindred soul, and has no trouble conversing at length with me. Nat's younger daughter is a firecracker with a temper to match, and the deepest gravelly voice; Nat was understandably concerned that their vibrant energy might be overwhelming for me this early in my healing journey. Fortunately, she had designated the furnished basement as my quiet zone.

The weather during our first evening was sunny and mild, so Nat and I headed out after dinner for a sunset walk with a stunning cliffside view of the Bow River. It was definitely a welcome outing to get some fresh air and gentle exercise, but after about an hour, I was ready to wave the white flag. My stamina was still an issue, but particularly so in those early days. Still, considering what I'd been experiencing, I was living up to my new hashtags: #MightyMo and #cancerthriver.

I had mentioned to Nat that I'd wanted to attend a Kundalini Yoga session, so she dropped me off, went to a café, and retrieved me later. It was my first teacher-led yoga class in months, and I wasn't certain how my stamina would be. Fortunately, the sequence—called a kriya—wasn't overly physically demanding as they sometimes can be, and was in fact one that I had practiced and taught several times over the past several years. It felt incredible to get back to the physical practice of Kundalini Yoga, as I'd been focussed primarily on the powerful healing and manifesting meditations associated with this tradition. Since March, I had been doing super-gentle movements such as Cat-Cow, Spinal Flex, Sufi Grinds (a type of pelvic/waist roll), Spinal Twist, and the straddle version of Life Nerve Stretch: all of which are dynamic but invite slow to moderate pacing and which serve as sufficient warm-ups for sitting in meditation. But I hadn't been practicing any full kriyas, so this class was entirely welcome.

Nat and I headed to visit my younger sis, Jocelyn, who lives in the 'burbs. We had arranged that Joce would shave my head entirely, as my lovely "do" that my former student, Angie, had given me back in April was suffering due to additional hair loss. After enjoying our lunch, we got down to the business of setting up the home-based barber shop. Fortunately, Joce is highly skilled at cutting hair; I'm sure she was a stylist in another lifetime! She cut the bulk of what was left and then took the clippers to clean up my scalp. I loved how I looked bald, but now have a complete understanding why bald folks wear hats most of the time! I was so easily chilled to begin with; now with no insulation on my head, I was definitely in need of a head covering.

Thursday evening I got the chance to meet a dear friend and former co-worker for dinner. Laurene was going to be heading to Bali in late summer to do her 200-hour Yoga Teacher Training as she'd been asked to teach Yoga at her school the following year. Between hearing more about that, plus answering all of her questions for me, I was pooped as our evening drew to a natural close. We walked back to Nat's place and said our farewells.

The primary reason for my trip to Calgary was happening on Friday night, May 31st. Back in March, I'd seen ads on Facebook about prolific author and spiritual teacher, Carolyn Myss coming to Calgary and I jumped at the chance to see her live. I had been deeply impacted by her mid-1990s book, *Anatomy of the Spirit,* which I'd found when I was going through a particularly heart-breaking, soul-searching time living in Alaska while on a year off. That book spoke so deeply to my lifelong spiritual searching for answers. I bought two tickets and was fairly easily able to convince Nat to join me.

Being raised as a polite Canadian, I was initially taken aback by how blunt Carolyn Myss was, though I grew to appreciate how unwilling she was to put up with anyone's "B.S." as she called it. I took lots of notes on my phone (It was that night that I heard for the first time about the relationship between grand mal seizures (as I'd had), Theresa of Avila's experience (as I'd had), and what Myss referred to as Mysticism Disorder, which has been studied and distinguished from a mental illness/disorder. Her talk had so many synchronicities relating to what I'd been experiencing and continue to experience. I loved that she repeatedly mentioned the importance of forgiveness, of prayer ("Pray like you're crazy!"), to appreciate the love we have in our life and not to be afraid to ask for guidance. She acknowledges that this is a powerful time of transition and evolution, which I was definitely feeling so very strongly, as I know so many others were as well. Towards the end of her talk, she mentioned that we are now creatures of 51% energy and

49% matter, which I found intriguing, as I embraced the concept that we are vibratory energetic beings.

I was on a flight back to Yellowknife on Sunday morning, excited to see my husband soon. My first five-day round of chemo (at 75% max dosage) would begin that night.

Chapter 10

Miracles Do Happen

Chemo Legs and Reintegration

MY RETURN TO Yellowknife heralded the first round of my at-home dosing of my chemo pills. This first round was not without its issues, mostly due to my naiveté and Robert's and my lack of knowledge on how to procure said meds. We had not been informed by my insurance company that a Pre-Authorization Form would need to be filled out and approved by them prior to my Temozolomide/Temodal being covered by insurance. Thus, when Robert went to pick up my chemo, he was charged $2,500! When we submitted the receipt for reimbursement, it was denied with little clarification until he called them. They initially mailed us the incorrect form and then attempted to blame us for filling in the wrong form after we waited a month to hear from them. Bureaucracy drives me crazy when I am healthy! At the time, it very nearly put me over the edge into the abyss of total despair. After being denied reimbursement a second time despite filling in the correct form, I found myself in a heap on the floor sobbing inconsolably. As it turned out, Robert had checked off the incorrect box after being asked if I had completed a concurrent radiation/chemo protocol. That is exactly what I had done but he misunderstood the term so checked off the "no" box. Once we all realized the error made, we were informed that we had been approved. Though it took two months longer than it needed to, the insurance company reimbursed us for the first two rounds of chemo that Robert had paid for out of pocket.

My naiveté with the first round was due to the belief that since I didn't bother taking the anti-emetic medication during my six-week concurrent radiation/chemo and didn't experience nausea, I would be fine not taking it before taking my first dose of 275 mg of TMZ (aka Temodal)—I could *not* have been more wrong! I spent over three hours puking every twenty to thirty minutes that first night. I took my Ondansetron like a good girl from then on, along with a dose of my CBD/THC oil. This first round was 150 mg higher in dose than what I had taken during my six-week stint, which would explain why I found my head in the toilet much of the first night. My remaining five rounds were even higher: 355 mg. And truly, the worst of my side effects of the chemo appeared to be what I came to call "chemo legs", as by day three of each five-day round, my legs felt like lead and I had no stamina whatsoever. Since the dog still needed walking and my husband had to work, I remained the primary dog walker. On a positive note, it always felt great to get outside, even if I had to walk a lot slower than I was accustomed to, and to take a short break on my way up the hill back to the condo.

Soon after, I was interviewed by Ollie Williams, one of the founding reporters of our local *Cabin Radio*. One of the other founding members, Jesse Wheeler, is also a former student and Facebook friend, and had reached out to me back in March after reading one of my long-winded "full confession"-type posts. At the time, I told him that I was not ready to go entirely public on that scale. But by late May, I let Jesse know that I was ready, especially now that I was home. He was not able to be present, so delegated the interview to Ollie. It was a live interview with a follow-up written online article. I have no problem with being interviewed nor with public speaking, which I fully recognize is one of my gifts. I thoroughly enjoyed how genuinely interested Ollie was and found him incredibly easy to chat with.

Also available online is a *My Yellowknife Now* article based on an interview with reporter Emelie Peacock. She and I spent almost an hour talking. Based on that long interview, Emelie crafted what I thought was a fair and positive article.

I had an in-person, free healing session with friend and former neighbour, Renee Fougere, who is trained in reiki. With my permission, she had done several distance reiki sessions on me while I was in Edmonton, keeping in regular contact over Messenger to share what she was picking up. The day after my *Cabin Radio* interview, I headed to her house on Latham Island, where she had a room with a massage table set up. Almost three hours later, exhausted and overwhelmed by the generosity of her gift, I headed home, ready for a much-needed nap and time to integrate all that she had shared with me and to begin the "homework" she'd given me: for example, to get back to my painting!

I had another energy healing session with Jillian, which, as usual, was very powerful and requires a woo woo alert, as she and the Record Keepers worked on what's called a "Soul Retrieval" that involved cleaning, reconnecting, and sealing the following parts of my body: my feet, knees, heart, and head. I was informed that the cancer was related to what is missing (though I will admit I didn't really grasp what was meant by that).

In a past life, during Egyptian times, I had apparently experienced a mummification process whereby my heart was removed from my chest cavity. As a result, my whole heart needed reconstruction and reintegration from that timeline. At that point, Archangel Uriel (best known as the Archangel of Forgiveness) appeared saying: "I come in peace. I bring you love and blessings from the Prime Creator." After more work to resolve some of my deeply held trust and safety issues, Uriel then said, "May this give you the solid foundation you've been missing." I was informed that I do not have to fear anything—no one will take anything from me, and I don't need to feel like I'm being punished. From my past life in Egypt, I was blaming myself for the theft of my heart, but I was since forgiven. I was encouraged to shine like the beautiful, brilliant human being that I am.

In yet another timeline, there was a violent attack to my head with an axe and a hammer. There was more healing work to be done, but not during this session. What the Record Keepers and guides then worked on was pulling energetic poisons out of my stomach, balancing the bacteria in the cell walls of my intestine to allow absorption and to balance the acidity and flora in my eliminative organs. Given how hard chemo is on the body and the digestive and eliminative systems, I appreciated the time spent there.

One common area—aside from my brain and heart—that is worked on each session is my throat, which was feeling perpetually constricted. We worked on softening and creating a general expansion both physically and energetically. I had an energetic lasso/noose around my neck as I was picking up on Robert's fear and allowing it to restrict me and tighten my "noose". I was asked to make a declaration to break the cycle: "I do not allow nor permit this lasso or noose to restrict me any longer from speaking and living my Truth. I return it to Source." I was informed that whenever I notice this happening again I was to call in the elements (earth, water, fire, air, and ether) to resolve the restriction, and specifically to use my intuition to know which of the elements to use most effectively. That day, we used fire to burn off the energetics and cut the cords using a sword-like action. Until recently, I still experienced what I liken to an "inflammation" in my throat chakra, so my interpretation is that I still need to work on speaking my truth and expressing my needs.

We also worked on my energetic solar plexus (third chakra) and third eye (sixth chakra) using the element of fire to restore my personal will, keep the flames burning, and allow the embers of the truth to be stoked. There was more work done in terms of the use of Light Languages; but I was told to rest and then practice my own activation of all of the parts that had been part of the Soul Retrieval. I was to ask the Creator, the Record Keepers, and my guides to bring back healing energy to those pieces returned. I was exhausted after our session and took time to rest and integrate all that had transpired.

I had been asked to speak at the upcoming local Brain Tumour Walk that weekend Luckily, the day dawned sunny and mild enough to wear a single layer by midday. Hosted by the Yellowknife Chapter of the Brain Tumour Foundation of Canada, I had managed to raise $1000 in a short period of time for the cause, thanks to the generosity of friends and family. I registered as an individual as opposed to being part of a team and was joined in the five-kilometre walk by my husband. Because it was in Yellowknife, I knew at least half of the people participating, which made my giving a ten-minute speech not too nerve-wracking. I shared the highlights of my journey to date, focusing on my mindset, and my decision to approach this experience from a place of "curious fascination", feeling fully confident that I'd not only survive but would continue to thrive.

The walk was hot and I over-extended myself. I should have turned around, but stubbornly completed the entire five km, which for me felt more like a ten km. We did not stay for the barbeque, as there was nothing I could eat there anyway, and I recognized my need to rest. I am looking forward to participating with Team #MightyMo in this year's walk if it happens.

Spring into Summer

I spent much of the remainder of June writing my speech to share with the Grad Class of 2019, their friends and families, and my coworkers and my family. I took a break from writing that Sunday, as I had a brilliant henna tattoo artist, Pasqueline Greau, coming over that day to draw what is called a henna crown on my bald skull. She spent three hours drawing a crown of sunflowers. I had chosen the sunflower design because of its importance in my family. When Luke had died five years prior, everyone in attendance at his Celebration of Life received a packet of sunflower seeds that had a photo of Luke on it with the instructions to please plant the seeds in June. Since then, I cannot look at a sunflower without being filled with unconditional love and cherished memories of Lukey.

As a result of the incredible generosity reflected in the GoFundMe contributions, my parents and all three of my sisters were coming to Yellowknife the final week of June and staying for several days. I was both excited and anxious about the latter, as I was unsure as to how the family dynamics were going to work given that it's a very rare event that all six of us are together in healthy times, not to mention when I'm so easily over-stimulated. I had made lodging arrangements for everyone, with Mom and Dad staying in our room for a night whilst Robert and I slept on the Murphy bed in my yoga and meditation room. They then moved in with dear and generous friends of ours: Jacqueline DeCoutere and Roger Soloudre. I farmed out my siblings, except Kirst, to other generous friends for a couple of nights. She stayed with us. Even though we did not spend our nights all together, our daytime and evening hours were plentiful given that we had just celebrated the Summer Solstice the Friday before. I do so love living in the Land of the Midnight Sun.

Grad was the next day for École Sir John Franklin High School. That morning, Paco returned to add bling to my henna crown, with the addition of fuchsia pink glitter washable glue and sticky "diamond gems". I was thrilled with the effect While my crown was drying, I asked Kirst to listen to my speech which moved her to tears. I had read it to the rest of the family the night before, just to get a sense of how long it would take me to read out loud but also to get any feedback from them. After weeks of mulling over what bits of "wisdom" I would choose to share with the Grad Class of 2019, my speech was entitled "One Journey, Many Paths." I used the numeral one instead of spelling it out because of its symbolism in Ten Body Kundalini Yoga numerology as representing the Soul Body. I elected to focus on two "Top Five" lists: the first was a list of five things to give up, which I elucidated in reverse order as: 5) Give up the need to be perfect; 4) Give up the need to be right; 3) Give up jealousy, envy, and holding on to resentments; 2) Give up self-judgment and fear; and 1) Give up trying to be everything to everyone. The second top five list was all about living up to their potential. I included the following advice: 5) Release limiting beliefs and adopt liberating beliefs; 4) Nourish ourself (aka self-care); 3) Adopt an "attitude of gratitude"; 2) Be kind and love yourself first; and 1) Be courageous. I shared personal examples plus some of the wisdom I'd read or listened to in both Top Five lists.

When it came time for my speech, I will admit to having some nerves, but once I got started, things flowed easily. People laughed when I meant for them to, and many in the crowd were moved to tears. It was my turn for tears when—upon completion—thunderous applause arose and people leapt to their feet giving me a standing ovation that seemed to go on and on. Blushing profusely, smiling broadly—if tearily—and giving a rather embarrassed but humble curtsy, I made my way down the stairs off the stage and shakily found my seat. After the ceremony when chairs were being cleared away in preparation for the requisite dances, I wandered around, giving and receiving hugs and kudos. There were a few photos with students taken. But with my family patiently waiting and not as emotionally invested in the Grad Class as I was, they wanted to get home as it had been an exceptionally long day.

The day after Grad dawned sunny but incredibly windy—and it felt a bit like early fall! I had let my family know prior to their arrival that we would have a photo shoot, so that they could decide what they wished to wear for the photos. I'd hired the incomparably sweet and uber-talented Hannah Eden: a transplanted English rose of a young woman who is as brainy as she is beautiful. Upon meeting her, my family was totally charmed by her diminutive stature but outgoing and easygoing personality and adept ability to get us to do whatever she thought would work best to capture our time together. We got some fantastic photos, to be sure, but even better were the gut-busting giggles! We are all reminded of that windy session on the Precambrian Shield in behind our condo whenever we look at the photos. I surprised Mom and Dad, and each of my sisters with wrapped canvas prints for Christmas. One of the photos that each of them received was my favourite one of the four of us; the other was my fave of each sis with me.

Photo by Hannah Eden Photography

More memories were created later that day, when we all piled into a Twin Otter float plane, along with my dear friend Deb, to fly to Blachford Lake Lodge to spend three nights at this awe-inspiring remote fly-in ecolodge 100 km east of Yellowknife. It was my eighth trip there, even more for Robert, and Deb's fifth or sixth trip. For Kirst, it was her second trip, as she had joined me and a wonderful crew for the second Kundalini Yoga Women's Retreat that I had co-hosted there along with Dev Suroop Kaur and Devinder Kaur in September 2018: we'd called it, "Elemental: Earth, Water, Wind, Fire, and Spirit." For Mom, Dad, Joce, and Mel, they would finally be able to get a first-person understanding of why I am so enamoured with this beautiful location in the wilderness of the Canadian sub-arctic.

I was on day two of my second round of chemo on the day of our arrival, so I was entirely grateful to have Old Trappers Cabin that Robert and I shared for privacy. Kirst and Deb shared Beaver Lodge, which they loved, and Mel and Joce shared Eagle's Nest. We had Mom and Dad stay in the main lodge so that neither of them would have to concern themselves with maneuvering climbing over any rocks, especially given the state of Dad's back and knee from a recent fall. Honestly, I think the man forgets he is in his eighties! Both he and Mom were grateful for their main lodge accommodations, and Dad quickly settled into reading all about the lodge's history.

Normally, summertime is ideal to make use of the lodge's kayaks and SUP boards, as well as making use of their several motorized boats for sightseeing or fishing. But given the high and cool winds, our time on the water was more limited but no less enjoyable, provided we dressed accordingly. Mel and Kirst did get out in the kayaks on a beautiful calm and sunny evening, thoroughly entertaining themselves with their awkward efforts exiting the water crafts an hour later. The property has a hot tub overlooking the lake and a wood-fired sauna in the woods close to the lakeshore. All of us except Dad made use of the hot tub, but only Deb and Kirst got into the sauna, followed by a courageous dunk in the bone chilling Blachford Lake. I was feeling exhausted most of my time there, so chose not to do the hiking I'd normally do, electing instead to either nap on one of the leather sofas in front of the woodstove, or head down to our cabin to rest in bed, also with the woodstove lit and cozy. There is never a shortage of food here, and it included some homemade baking, some of which was actually "Mo-friendly".

Aside from two personable and fit fellows from Switzerland, we were the sole guests for three nights at the lodge, which was surprising but welcome. On our first night, Kris, our lodge manager, got a fire going in the tipi and we all trekked the relatively short but potentially tricky trail to hang out and swap stories.

The day after our arrival, Joce had us all apply silly Canada Day temporary tattoos, as it was July 1st: Canada Day. Dad applied his smack in the middle of his forehead, which put us into fits of laughter at his light-heartedness. We passed our days doing whatever we felt like: reading, napping, listening to Dad strum the ukulele, whilst Mel and Mom played cribbage and other card games. Kirsten, Deb, and Mel did their fair share of hiking. There was enough room in the main lodge and environs to give one another space if and when deemed necessary.

Our final night, we gathered near the lakeshore in front of Old Trappers Cabin to have a campfire, roast marshmallows to make s'mores, and enjoy the waning hours together. Dad chose to stay in the lodge. The next day, and before we were necessarily ready, it was time to head back to town. Mel, who has a phobia of flying, was understandably reticent about hopping back on the twin otter. But luckily, the pilot is highly accomplished and experienced and a retired RCMP pilot as well as a long-time friend. I knew we were in great hands and tried to relieve Mel's anxiety—not entirely successfully. It was a smooth flight home: certainly, less choppy than our flight to the lodge and within a half-hour of taking off, we were landing on Yellowknife Bay and pulling into the Air Tindi dock. We gathered our luggage, and dropped Deb off before driving to the condo.

Healing Continues at Home

Once everyone had departed, it was time for me to get back to more treatment. I had a follow-up appointment with Dr. Shahin Moslehi after our initial intake appointment. He asked me: "Can I call you Mo? Everyone here seems to call you Mo!" I laughed and said, "Of course! But what shall I call you?" Without hesitating, he responded, "Sha!" And so, our friendship began. Twice a week for the following three weeks, I would be hooked up to gradually increasing doses of intravenous Poly-MVA and DCA, both of which are detailed in the book, *Outside the Box Cancer Therapies: Alternative Therapies That Treat and Prevent Cancer,* by integrative Drs. Mark Stengler and Paul Anderson. These sessions lasted anywhere from two to three hours and given that they are considered alternative approaches, they are not covered by insurance. Generously, Sha indicated that for all my sessions, he would only ever charge me for the appointment time and the wholesale cost of the treatments. That also included the mistletoe therapy (Helixor A/Vicosan A) which I began by self-injection in mid-July. Despite the generous deal Sha was offering, my treatments still cost me thousands of dollars. I cannot imagine what it would have cost me if I lived south of the border.

The month of July also entailed a great deal of communication and phone interviews with the individual case worker assigned to me by the insurance company based in Calgary: a Reimbursement Specialist as well as a Nurse Case Manager, both based in Toronto. They assisted me in arranging my chemo to be sent up from a pharmacy in Edmonton, as we were no longer allowed to use our local Shoppers Drug Mart. The chemo had to be expedited up to Yellowknife each of the four remaining rounds, but the pharmacy couldn't send it until they'd received the order from CCI after my blood work results. This left very little time between placing the order and when I was to start the next round of chemo, which caused some unnecessary stress.

I had another session with Jillian booked for the following week which once again seemed to revolve around the issues of trust, self-love, worthiness, allowing the flow of abundance, and, of course, self-forgiveness. I was encouraged to break through the barriers of self-doubt and recognize my intuitive abilities and understand all forms of abundance: the most essential form of which being love. I was told, "You are a Divine Angel of God. You can release these feelings of having to hold everyone else's energy. God forgives you, as there is nothing to forgive." I was informed that my perceived lack of self-worthiness has to do with my inability to forgive myself and goes back many lifetimes. There is shame involved and I was prompted to recognize that whatever happened in those lifetimes no longer served me and could be released: that it was not mine and that I was to release all self-judgment to Source.

I understand that this is likely a big stretch for many readers. I'm a believer, through and through. In many of my lifetimes, there had been a good deal of torture; I'd felt like I deserved it because I believed I had let God down. My legs had been dismembered in one such lifetime. In the present timeline I had to help clear the energy in my legs, which interestingly were shaky even before our session had started. I had to make the conscious choice to remove and clear the energy that no longer served me. In the same session, the Record Keepers advised me that I had multiple energetic arms, like some of the Hindu deities (Nataraja, a Hindu deity, comes to mind). These six arms exist on the multidimensional plane and actively fan out, practicing a number of different mudras (yogic hand positions). I was then given a declaration for self-forgiveness: though after repeating it as asked, I no longer recall what was said. The Record Keepers also described the image of my being a Phoenix rising with my wings of fire with the prompting to, "Rise, rise, rise!" Just before wrapping up this session, Jillian channelled the ancient Egyptian goddess Isis who said, "You are a child of the Divine/You are whole and complete as is/May you go in peace with love in your heart." That made my jaw drop with excitement.

Cause for Celebration

On the day of our tenth wedding anniversary, July 18th, Nat flew up from Calgary. I was thrilled that she had prioritized coming up to witness Robert's and my vows renewal, happening out at "SoLaCe" on Saturday, July 20th. Robert and Nat headed to the cabin on Friday

110

morning with Tillie, and I joined them later. I had a phone appointment with my insurance company, followed by my IV Poly-MVA and DCA with my naturopathic doc, the latter of which took over two hours.

It was a glorious summer evening, and once at the cabin with Robert and Nat, we ate our dinner outdoors and Nat and I got out onto the water: I was in one of the kayaks and Nat was on my inflatable SUP. Tillie followed us both along shore and swam a good way too. It was a wonderful way to introduce Nat more fully to my happy place. The next morning, we were fairly occupied getting set up for the ceremony, which would be informal. The weather forecast was sunny and hot, so before it got too hot, Nat and I, and Tillie of course, headed out onto the water towards the Cameron River Channel, with Nat and I in kayaks and Tillie swimming and running along the shoreline.

Robert took charge of being the water taxi, ferrying a hand-picked number of family and long-time friends of ours—mainly local—but others who had travelled for the occasion. We made sure to get a group photo before the day was over.

Robert and I laughing on rocks
Photo by Hannah Eden Photography

Deb served as the emcee, and once everyone was settled in their chairs on the front deck, she invited each person to introduce themselves and tell a story of how they had met either Robert, me, or both. Hilarity ensued! Considering Robert had friends there that he'd grown up with in Hudson Bay, Saskatchewan decades ago, there were some great tales told.

Robert and I had agreed to read our original vows and then add an update, not revealing what we had composed to the other until reading them in front of the small crowd gathered. I was beyond moved by Robert's vulnerability. As someone who is entirely unaccustomed to speaking in front of a crowd, no matter how small, Robert bravely opened his heart to tearfully share words of unconditional love and recommitment. It broke my heart wide open to listen and attempt to absorb. I have watched that video so often since.

Similar to our original wedding ceremony, we told folks that we didn't wish to receive any gifts, as their presence was more than enough, which a few folks ignored and brought a small gift. There were some delicious appetizers and sides provided by all, along with the beverages, barbecued steaks, and chicken that Robert generously supplied.

Miracles Do Happen

Robert and I were up early on Wednesday morning, as our flight to Edmonton was departing at 6:00 am. I was packing to be away for two and a half weeks, as after my MRI and follow-up oncology outpatient exam, I was going to be travelling onward to Toronto to visit family and friends for the weekend and then to New Brunswick to spend nine days with my parents, my youngest sister Melanie, and her two daughters.

En route to Edmonton, I began listening to the audiobook, *Radical Remissions: Surviving Cancer Against All Odds*, by Kelley A. Turner, PhD. I couldn't get enough of the happy-ending stories of real-life cancer survivors who had through various approaches managed to heal themselves from their serious and sometimes terminal diagnoses. At one point, I was sitting with tears streaming, as the story I was listening to feature a man who healed himself from the same type of brain tumour that I still have. There has since been a ten-part docuseries released by Hay House in partnership with the author of the book in early 2020. I watched every episode and loved them all. Each episode focused on one component that Turner's research had shown was a commonality in all radical remission survivors. What I was particularly enthused about was that I believe that I possess all ten of these qualities too. They are:

- Empowering Yourself
- Radically Changing Your Diet
- Releasing Suppressed Emotions
- Increasing Positive Emotions
- Bringing Exercise and Movement into Your Life
- Having Strong Reasons for Living
- Deepening Your Spiritual Connection Practice
- Using Herbs and Supplements
- Following Your Intuition
- Embracing Social Support

My decision to approach everything about my healing journey from a place of curious fascination continued and the only person present with nervous energy was Robert. Kirsten was very nervously awaiting our contact. My MRI was scheduled for that afternoon, with blood work to be taken afterward. We would get the results of my exam the following day. It was a "hurry up and wait" situation, as they were running a half hour behind, which did nothing but raise my husband's stress levels and heighten his anxiety. In contrast, I was quite relaxed.

Truthfully, the MRI was far noisier than I remembered, despite wearing the heavy-duty headphones they provide, and that it took longer than I anticipated. I spent the twenty-five minutes focused on my breath and the rhythm of the beeps and thunks of the machine, visualizing my tumour having shrunk. By the time it was over, I was almost as relaxed as I had been in any of my floats.

The following day, I had my next VAHT (harp) session with Bev Ross, which really assisted in allowing me to sink into a full and complete relaxation: body, mind, and spirit.

We were expecting to see Dr. Easaw, but instead my new nurse practitioner came in—beaming—introducing himself saying that we hadn't yet met in person but had spoken on the phone whilst I was hiking one morning. We shook hands and I asked him for his permission to FaceTime with my twin sister while he shared the results, with which he had no problem. He could not stop smiling as he then asked, "So, have you heard anything about your results yet?" Of course, I responded that we had not. He shook his head and said, "I have to pull this up on the monitor, because I have never seen anything like this in my life! You'll have to see it for yourself."

He pulled up my original brain image from March, when the tumour truly was the monster the neurosurgeon had biopsied. I'll admit to experiencing a shock when I saw it clearly with my own eyes. It was gigantic! On March 8th, 2019, my GBM measured 3.5 x 3.2 x 4.9 cm. The nurse practitioner then pulled up the image of my scan from the day before and the tumour appeared miniscule in comparison: measuring 1.5 x 1.7 x 2.9 cm! All three of us in the room—and Kirsten on the phone—were gobsmacked by this unexpected and seemingly miraculous result. I think I embarrassed the NP when I spontaneously exclaimed, "Omigosh, I feel like hugging you right now!" to which he responded perhaps uncomfortably, "Well, you could if it'd make you feel better." I hugged my husband instead, but I certainly gave the nurse practitioner a much warmer handshake at the end of our meeting.

Robert and I floated out of the exam room, signed off with Kirst and set to make a few phone calls, first and foremost to my parents and Robert's mom. I texted my other two sisters, and my friends Nat, Lisa, and Debbie. We stopped by the Records desk to get a copy of the report, which read in part: "The left cingulate gyrus complex enhancing mass with cystic/necrotic areas has significantly decreased in size...resolution of midline shift...significant interval decrease in left frontal vasogenic edema." Walking back towards the hotel, we stopped for a snack and a celebratory glass of prosecco at Earls restaurant. Robert did the math: my tumour had shrunk from 54.88 cubic centimeters to 7.39 cubic centimeters. That is a decrease in volume of 86.52%—truly "mind-blowing." Once we got back to our hotel room, I shared a message on social media. The response was overwhelming. It was quite humbling, and I allowed for tears of joy as the responses continued to pour in.

Chapter 11

A New Reality

Celebrations

MY COUSIN, JEREMY, picked me up at Pearson International and was kind enough to drive me to the pharmacy where my prescription for my DCA capsules were awaiting pickup. He then took me to my beloved friend's Komal Bhasin's townhouse in the artsy Queen West neighbourhood where I would be staying for three nights prior to flying to Saint John, New Brunswick. I loved introducing Jeremy to Komal and her spouse, Sumit, as I knew they would hit it off. Komal and Sumit consider me family; their guest room is referred to as "my room", though I'm certain I'm not their only occasional overnight guest.

I have a large base of friends and family that live in the greater Toronto area and had reached out to some of my high school friends. Four of them were able to join me for dinner that night. We had a great time reconnecting, as for some, it had been over thirty years since we'd seen one another. Admittedly, given that it was a summer's evening in a popular urban neighbourhood, I was soon overstimulated. I found the volume of conversation quite challenging but dealt with it because the company and the food was fabulous. Better yet, the four of my long-time high school pals treated me to dinner!

My cousin Jeremy was picking me up around 3:00 pm to take us to his parents' home where they occupy the top flat of a four-storey mansion that my eldest cousin, Tony, owns with his family.

My Uncle Court—Mom's brother—and my Aunt Sandra, warmly welcomed me, along with my cousin, Michael, who I had not seen in at least thirty years and his younger brother, Christian. Jeremy's wife, Beth, was also there with their baby. It was a gorgeous summer afternoon, so Chris and Michael and I spent an hour in the pool and then we all relaxed with some delicious fresh fruit, veggies, cheeses, and beverages from the comfort of the adjoining outdoor cabana. Once everyone dried off, we took pictures and ventured out for dinner. Our crowd took up an entire quarter of the space, I am quite certain. It was there that Uncle Court revealed that his lymphoma had returned after an eleven-year remission. He was very laissez-faire about it, which made me think that he thought that I already knew. I did not, and was upset by the news but was hesitant to ask too many questions lest he think I was being too obnoxiously forward.

The next day I landed in Saint John and I was greeted by my extended family, some of whom I hadn't seen for a couple of years. It is a family tradition to gather as many relatives as possible to greet incoming family members at the airport. It was especially poignant this time, and most of us were crying.

We spent my first evening around the firepit in the backyard, roasting marshmallows to make s'mores. Sadly, I was not indulging, as I had adopted the ketogenic diet in mid-July and thus no grains and no sugar for me. Though I do love roasting marshmallows, so I enjoyed roasting a couple for my nieces. My parents live in the house that Dad built, and where I grew up from four years old until I moved out at eighteen. There is an inground pool that he built back when Kirsten and I were six or seven that was converted to salt water relatively recently. I took full advantage of it not being chlorine-based and swam laps on a nearly daily basis during my visit. We entertained all cousins and friends wishing to visit, with the understanding that I was just finishing my third round of chemo and required a lot of rest and limited noise.

I practiced yoga and meditation daily, either in the living room, outdoors on the back patio, or at the local yoga studio owned by dear friends, Jason McLean and Stephanie Downey. Yoga Haus is a gorgeous, light-filled space on the main street linking my hometown of Quispamsis to Rothesay.

There were highlights of my visit home, all of which included memorable moments with lifelong friends and, of course, family. One highlight was certainly the annual potluck that Mom and Dad host, scheduled to coincide with when at least one of the Tonge girls is home. Begun in 1995, the annual party is quite the shindig, with well over one hundred people invited each year.

Mom and Dad provided the homemade strawberry shortcake and booze. As well, Dad always provided thirty pounds of mussels, cooking them in a gigantic pot in the backyard according to his labour-intensive but delicious recipe. Despite a province-wide shortage, we found some to enjoy at the party.

Once dressed, refreshed, and eager to connect with the family and friends who had surrounded me with their loving prayers of support, healing, and generosity with the GoFundMe account, I made my way out into the backyard and connected with as many people as I could. After availing myself of a plateful of mussels, barbequed chicken, and any salads that I could eat, Dad asked me to make a speech. I did so—with sincere gratitude—thanking everyone for all they had so generously provided me and my family over the previous six months.

Several of my school pals, some of whom Kirst and I have been close with since kindergarten, made a point of attending, and I tried to get group photos with as many as possible.

I was due to depart New Brunswick on the Friday and for the first time in memory, I wasn't feeling ready to say goodbye. It turned out to be the final time I saw my Uncle Ken, as he died in the autumn of 2019. Along with my other relatives, he and my Auntie Ann came to the airport to say goodbye. I can feel good that my last communication with my Uncle Ken were the words, "I love you."

New Reality Sets In

The remainder of August consisted of doctor's appointments—both with my family doctor as well as my naturopathic doctors in Yellowknife and by phone in Kelowna—my monthly blood work, hosting a Full Moon Meditation at Collective Soul Space, a couple of tea dates and lunch dates with friends, and round four of chemo which caused some digestive upset but nothing overly serious. I had a session with Jillian on August 29th, the day before the anniversary of Lukey's passing, which is typically a tough day: five years of missing him, every single day. What helps to sustain me is knowing that he is still watching over us.

The work I was doing with Jillian continued to revolve around healing my self-limiting beliefs: the deep wounds of shame, of not feeling like enough—peeling away the next layer like an onion. Also, I was learning that I needed to tune into the energy of my womb—my Divine Feminine—to tap more completely into the flow of my creativity and the required expression of it so that I could continue to heal.

In this particularly powerful session, there was a segment of working through what I had termed "residual resentment" when asked what my intention was for our hour together; but I was soon comically corrected by the Record Keepers that this resentment and anger that I was harbouring were more than residual. I was suppressing the true size of this resentment which was, in fact, deep-seated. An image came through of my energy body standing opposite a person with arrows going back and forth between us. They explained that what I was holding onto goes beyond space and time: that the trigger was in other timelines. Fortunately, I was also told that what I healed on that day would be healed in both people as well as going beyond this realm. In the other timeline, I had been betrayed by this person and burned at the stake while they had been spared. At that time, I had asked, "Why are you allowed get away with this? Why do you get to live?" This energy blueprinted in my subtle body. I was directed to heal and release this resentment through the element of fire through which it was initially created. As I sobbed, I was asked to tune into my heart centre and recognize that my anger and resentment came from a place of Divine Love, as in, "Why don't you love yourself as much as I love you?" I was then reminded of something that I have only recently begun to embrace wholeheartedly: that all souls have their own paths to follow. As much as I want this person to make changes in their life, it is none of my business! This is such a good lesson for me, and undoubtedly others, to recognize: the only person I can truly change is myself.

Regarding my creative expression, I was informed that I needed to release my belief that it needed to be a certain way; I needed to recognize the depth and breadth of my talent and what the Record Keepers called my raw potential. I needed to start experimenting with what my soul wanted to create, not what I've been conditioned to do. That felt intimidating! An image of me in meditation with my eyes closed appeared, and I was encouraged by the Record Keepers to ask, "What does my soul want to create today?" and then to use my newly re-discovered intuition to come forth.

September was also a full month. I had returned to teaching twice-weekly classes at Collective Soul Space: "Mindful Movement and Meditation" on Mondays at lunch, and my longer "Kundalini Yoga for Stress Relief" class on Wednesdays. I also had regularly scheduled medical appointments, and blood work. For my next MRI, which took place in Edmonton in mid-September, I was accompanied by Robert and Kirsten who flew in from Abbotsford. I was 100% certain that there would be further evidence of dramatic shrinkage because I was so high-functioning and feeling so well! Thus, I really struggled with my disappointment when the results indicated that my tumour was stable, with indiscernible change in volume. Soon after, I was given a reality check by my ever-logical and loving twinnie, who said: "Mo, you have the most highly-aggressive form of brain tumour one could possibly have. The fact that there is no change in volume since July *is* an improvement, and great news!" When put that way, I was able to reconcile my feelings.

Return to the Temple

The absolute highlight of my autumn was a very special trip that I made to Greece, to a Women's Kundalini Yoga Retreat led by two friends with whom I'd organized two previous retreats: Devinder Kaur from Ottawa and Dev Suroop Kaur from Española, New Mexico. They were joined by a third instructor from Iceland who I connected with quickly, far more quickly than it took for me to learn how to pronounce her name: Ragnhildur Ragnarsdottir.

My functional nutritionist, Sara, and my primary ND, Sha, encouraged me to not worry about staying in ketosis once in Greece, but rather to eat joyfully all of the freshly homemade Greek food that I could. I complied with great gusto! I chose, however, to use my trusty lapis lazuli pendulum to "body douse" to see which foods would agree with me and my digestive system and which ones would not. Interestingly enough, it was in Greece that I discovered I could tolerate delicious Greek yogurt, freshly made kefir (a fermented dairy beverage full of probiotics and thus great for the gut), and goat and sheep cheese—even once back in Canada. After being off sugar of all kinds for two months, I threw caution to the wind as I got into the habit of drizzling some delicious local honey over top of my morning yogurt.

Landing almost an hour earlier than scheduled in Athens the morning of September 27th, I took a taxi to the winding narrow streets of the Plaka to the hotel where Dev Suroop and her sister, Susan Shulenberger were staying. I was not going to be able to check into my studio apartment that I had booked until later in the day, so we had time for a wonderful pre-retreat visit. We were thrilled to see one another. Dev Suroop confessed to me that she had been highly doubtful that I would make the trip given my diagnosis but was thrilled that I had. After I dropped off my bag and refreshed myself, the three of us meandered through some of the nearby shops.

Dev Suroop Kaur, Susie and I in Athens

We encountered three of the other retreat attendees (Devinder Kaur, her mom Josephine Finney, and Kathleen Ross) rather serendipitously on one of the tightly-packed streets of the Plaka. Electing to walk together to the Acropolis Museum, we spent over an hour perusing the relics and gorgeous sculptures of ancient times, capturing photos whenever and wherever allowed. We found an outdoor patio restaurant at which to enjoy a hearty lunch mid-afternoon, but my energy waned greatly as my jet lag set in. Dev Suroop, Susie, and I made our way back to their hotel so I could retrieve my luggage and take a cab to where I was staying in the Kolonaki neighbourhood. Traffic was horrendous, especially getting out of the Plaka, taking at least forty minutes for me to arrive at my destination to meet the gentleman who was going to show me my tiny apartment and give the ins and outs to how everything operated. I was going to be spending two nights in this sweet and stylishly modern studio apartment. I looked forward to exploring the neighbourhood a bit before departing to the island of

Karpathos, location of our "Return to the Temple" Women's Kundalini Yoga Retreat. But first, I needed sleep.

The next morning, I took advantage of the tiny balcony off the bedroom overlooking a small and shaded courtyard to enjoy my tea and small breakfast. I was excited to get out to walk around again after having had a good night's sleep. The heat of the day got progressively higher—despite being the end of September—but we were blessed to have shade in several places during our walk up the hill to the Acropolis. I had been there before with my mom in 2002 but was grateful to return. Sue and I were pleasantly surprised to have arrived on a day when admittance to all historical sites and museums in Athens was free; that was an unexpected treat. Because of that, however, the lineups were long, with security strongly urging everyone to keep moving. We felt a bit like herded cattle but made it to the Parthenon and through any areas not roped off. Despite the heat and the crowds, which I cannot even fathom they would have been like in summer, we were glad we went.

On the way back down, we perused a few hillside restaurants, choosing to stop at one in particular that had well-shaded outdoor seating. We chose well and thoroughly enjoyed our hearty Greek lunches. Parting ways soon after, I walked to the Temple of Olympian Zeus. Though the Parthenon is far better preserved, the Olympieion was also impressive, and I had read that in its day was a more monumental temple. As I continued on my walk back to the apartment, I came upon a small grassy park, where I decided to rest and meditate for a while to ground myself from the busyness of the day.

Within two minutes of my apartment, I happened upon Etherfloat, and decided to pop in to see if they had any openings; they did, and I returned two hours later to experience my first-ever Greek float experience. I was given a tour of this most impressive facility and encouraged to enjoy some locally-harvested tea and relax in the comfortable post-float seating area prior to my departure. It was exactly what I needed after a Transatlantic flight and two full days in the city of Athens. I was entertained by one of the co-owners of Etherfloat as we shared tea, water, and a surprisingly deep conversation.

I travelled solo to the airport the following day, quickly coming to the realization that taxis are not cheap in Athens. We departed on time to the island of Karpathos that afternoon. It was glorious to fly over the Aegean Sea and I recognized Santorini and Crete, two of the islands that I had visited with Mom in the autumn of 2002. As we approached the island of Karpathos, I'll admit to being surprised at its size; it was bigger than I had anticipated, though not nearly as big as Crete. Of course, I could have researched it prior to my trip, but chose not to, beyond going to the website of the retreat centre. It was a smooth landing and we were greeted by our retreat hosts: Kathrine Brustad and her partner, Elias Giano, who escorted us to the two passenger vans that would take us along the winding, narrow, and mountainous roads to Adia, the village where Kathy's Island Retreat is located. As we rounded the corner on the last few meters before the driveway, we caught sight of Kathy's Island Retreat. I soon realized that the pictures on the website only hinted at the jaw-dropping beauty of this retreat location and was particularly drawn to the outdoor studio platform that overlooked the Aegean Sea! We were given a welcoming freshly-squeezed juice upon our arrival and an orientation to the grounds. We were shown our rooms and then given a bit of freedom to continue to explore prior to dinner. I was gratified to have been given a single room, so that I could get the quiet that my brain needed.

The official opening of the retreat wouldn't be taking place until the following evening, and there were still one or two more people to arrive that day. The majority of us took advantage of the gorgeous sunny and breezy Monday to hike the twenty minutes along a narrow path that hugged the cliffside to a private rocky lagoon that was accessed by descending a handmade ladder that was more stable than it initially appeared. Even the adorable resident pooch, Lily, made the trek; in fact, she led the way, obviously accustomed to the path and descending the ladder! The water was a postcard gorgeous turquoise blue with white-crested waves rushing the rocky shore, inviting us to bob, float, and swim in its depths. The temperature was refreshingly divine.

There was also a rocky beach in the opposite direction that was easier to access: a ten-minute walk along a rarely travelled road that also featured a taverna on the way. Wee Lily would often accompany anyone heading there to swim, lounge, nap, and read during our break times and she would typically nap. There were some working dogs that we had to navigate around; however, they never got too close to us. Apparently, they had attacked sweet Lily in the past, but she was intrepid and smartly avoided them.

I was fortunate to have my room on the ground floor and elected to keep my balcony doors partly open at night with the mosquito net around my bed. I was often visited by the resident cat, aptly named Yoga: a purring machine, cuddly and very playful, especially in the early pre-dawn hours. He kept me entertained for the three nights that he chose to spend with me.

Karpathos at sunset October 2019

The days of the retreat were well-balanced. We had a delightful group opening on the Monday evening after dinner that allowed for getting to know one another better. Most participants were Canadian, with three from the U.S.A. We were also given a lovely booklet called *My Time* that outlined the format of the retreat with pages for journalling and included other important information such as how we opened and closed each session in the tradition of Kundalini Yoga and Meditation. Each day would focus on a different Greek goddess that we would learn a few stories about: Tyche (lady luck, prosperity and fortune); Aphrodite (love and beauty); Gaia (Mother Earth); Eos (dawn, hope of a brand new day); Athena (wisdom, poetry, art, and war strategy); Iris (rainbow, messenger of the gods, sea, and the sky); Rhea (nature, daughter of Gaia); and Nike (victory). We had an active Kundalini Yoga practice each morning from 7:30–8:30 that reflected the essence of the goddess of the day, followed by breakfast. We had a second practice that included a creative exploration activity from 11:00 am–1:00 pm followed by lunch from 1:30–2:30 pm. There was ample free time each afternoon before dinner at 7:00 or 7:30 pm, with two days set aside as excursion days. During this free time, we were encouraged to book an outdoor massage with our massage therapist, Frank: most renowned for regularly asking: "How you feel?" in a deep, heavily-accented—and thus quite sexy—tone of voice. We were also invited to go hiking, swimming, or just hang out—such freedom of choice!

Additionally, we had scheduled gentle practices and meditations each evening at 8:30 which occasionally featured a blissful gong "bath", readily inducing relaxation to then crawl into bed. The three teachers alternated their teaching slots throughout the day, which not only highlighted their different styles but also their strengths.

Our first excursion late in the afternoon on Wednesday, was to the ancient village of Olympos: a scenic series of homes and shops carved right into the mountainside, intentionally built to appear hidden from pirates, and until relatively recently, completely isolated except for boat access down the mountain. Most of the labyrinthian cobblestone streets in the historic village allow for pedestrian traffic only and were tricky to manoeuvre even on foot. We were encouraged by our retreat hosts, Kathrine and Elias, to shop in the tiny stores mostly owned and operated by charming elderly Greek ladies wearing traditional handmade headscarves. Several of us were fitted with our own headscarves, happy to invest in the local economy in the simplest of ways. Many retreat participants—myself included, also purchased small pieces of painted pottery, coloured glass Evil Eye pendants or keychains, and handwoven or hand-hewn leather crafts. We arrived at the top of the village in time to capture the sunset over the Aegean, which rivalled anything I had ever viewed. I climbed up some very narrow steps over a chapel to a flat rooftop to watch the sun sink below the horizon. We all gathered at a tiny restaurant for a casual and entertaining catered dinner before making our way back to the vans in the dark for the winding ride home down the mountain.

My group presentation was scheduled for the Thursday about which I was simultaneously excited and nervous. I had made some notes beforehand and had organized my presentation into three sections: "Pre-Diagnosis", "Diagnosis/Initial Treatment", and "Integrated Treatments and Life at Home". Dance breaks took place between each section, as dance had been such a huge part of my daily ritual and routine in the preceding months. Specifically, we boogied to upbeat songs from my "BT Dance Playlist".

In the first part, I spoke about my limiting beliefs (e.g. unworthiness, not good enough), my sensory overload and hypersensitivity (e.g. smells and sounds), anxiety, and depression. As well, I touched on my starting to receive what I called Signs from the Universe, in terms of number patterns and memes that would appear on my Instagram feed. In the second section, I spoke about my actual diagnosis and my reaction to it including my refusal to listen to my prognosis when asked, as I recognized that I was not my diagnosis, nor my prognosis. I detailed my approach regarding my mindset, coming from a place of curious fascination for each new experience which included getting fitted for my radiation mask. Including a description of my understanding how trauma played a role in my illness, I illustrated my need to shed the "issues in my tissues" on a physical and energetic level before I could find healing, describing my weight loss as evidence of the physical shedding and the energetic shedding through my work with Jillian and others practicing reiki on me. Above all, I highlighted my full-on faith and trust that I would heal, as I knew beyond a shadow of a doubt that the Universe had a far grander plan for me.

Naturally, I shared how the unanticipated and overwhelming level of support I had been receiving was helping me heal on all levels. I had been hesitant to share because I wanted to get a better sense of the group's receptivity. They were entirely on-board to hear more, so that I would have the opportunity on Saturday to do Part Two of my presentation for anyone who was genuinely interested; it would be as much of the spiritual and energetic woo woo stuff.

Our second excursion took place on Friday after our morning practice, when we went to Pigadia, the capital city of Karpathos, where we were encouraged once more to spend our euros to support the local economy and have lunch prior to driving to Amoopi Beach. Though a quaint harbour town with a population of 2500, personally, I would have preferred more time at the beach! It was a sunny and breezy afternoon, and the waves at Amoopi Beach were a blast to bob in for a while. I enjoyed a short stroll along the rocky path to a view of the larger beach nearby. Before I was ready, it was time to head back to Kathy's Island Retreat.

One of my favourite creative activities was when we picked a small stone on which we would then have our partner write a word they felt encapsulated our spirit. I was partnered with Dev Suroop, with whom I had several deep and revealing conversations over the past three years. She nailed it for me, writing the words, "empowered me" on my rock, using my favourite colours of markers! I keep the stone on my home yoga room window ledge, along with all of my crystals and semi-precious stones. Another of my favourite creative and memorable activities was creating the prayer flags. On one of our flags we wrote our name (I wrote my spiritual name: Dhanraj Kaur), setting it at one corner of our outdoor studio with the other flags. We all took the time that day and into the evening, to write one trait on each person's flag that we appreciated about them. Most messages on my flag used the words "inspire", "inspiration" and "blessed". I really enjoyed that process and reading mine after we were allowed to collect our flags made me teary with gratitude and love for my fellow retreatants.

Elias and Kathrine were such gracious hosts; I appreciated their attention to detail and their desire to make our retreat experience as worthwhile as possible. Dev Suroop celebrated her sixtieth birthday on one of our final nights, and Kathrine and Elias prepared a special dessert and sang "Happy Birthday" to her. They were then joined by Dev Suroop to sing karaoke, and we were invited to sing along. The karaoke continued more than one evening, with Elias and Kathrine leading us. As a professional musician and songstress, Dev Suroop skilfully serenaded us as well.

I was additionally grateful that Kathrine and Elias allowed us to stay extra nights for a reasonable fee both at the beginning and in my case, at the end of the official retreat, as I had booked my return flight for the day after everyone else was departing. They invited me to join them for dinner that night with the new crew of people that had arrived. I left Kathy's Island Retreat with mixed feelings. My taxi driver was a former professional soccer/football player and fluent in English, who made the forty-minute drive to the local airport fly by with his desire for conversation. On the one hand, I was grateful to have been so welcomed to this beautiful island retreat and was leaving with treasured memories. On the other hand, I felt ready to return home, despite what was going to be a shocking change of temperature. To me, feeling ready is always a good sign.

Chapter 12

"Brainiversary" Approaching

Return to the Body Temple

IF YOU ARE at all familiar with yoga, meditation, and other like-minded modalities, you have no doubt heard that we are encouraged to treat our physical body as a sacred temple: attentive to the food, liquids, and thoughts that we ingest, as well as the actions we take. That concept became more important to me as the weeks and months progressed on my healing journey. I minimized my consumption of alcohol once I became obviously symptomatic in January of 2019 and gave it up entirely in October as I had lost the taste for it. However, it was much more of a challenge to give up sugar, which primarily consisted of coconut palm sugar, maple syrup, and honey with minimal cane sugar as I had an intolerance to it. It took a few weeks to wean myself off of the delicious organic dark maple syrup and I gave away the large tub of raw Alberta honey that had been a fixture in our cupboard as well as what remained of my coconut sugar.

Once back from Greece, I recommitted fully to adopting the ketogenic diet, despite my inability to consume eggs. I had read in Mariam Kalamian's book, *Keto for Cancer: Ketogenic Metabolic Therapy as a Targeted Nutritional Strategy* in June and July, and readily admit that I am not as strict as her book recommends; I discovered that limiting myself to twenty net carbs a day is unfeasible for me without feeling like I am unnecessarily depriving myself. I function far better on forty to fifty net carbs per day. For folks unfamiliar with the term 'net' carbs, subtract the grams of fibre from the total carb content. Voila! In the realm of sweet treats I've learned how to make myself snacks such as

"Chocolate Fat Bombs", "Keto Chocolate Pecan Cookies" and "Keto Chewy Chocolate Chip Cookies" using erythritol and monk fruit as sugar substitutes, almond and coconut flours, raw organic cacao, nut and seed butters, and coconut oil or butter. I initially really missed the caramel cluster cashew ice cream that I was buying up until I committed to the keto diet. A small tub of it remained in the freezer until May 2020, when I finally recognized that the likelihood of my ever eating ice cream again was negligible. Robert made quick work of it once given the go-ahead!

On a healthier note, I have always really enjoyed my greens, so ate my fill of those along with as many lower carb vegetables as possible. The toughest food for me to limit, admittedly, is the amount of fruit that I consume. Once a week or so, I invite my husband to split an organic Granny Smith apple with me as an afternoon snack that I consume with some nut butter for fat and protein. I often add no more than one-third cup of berries to my Greek yogurt and green smoothies. Avocadoes, which I loved before, remain a staple, though I do try to pace myself and not eat them every day lest I develop an intolerance. I learned about ten years ago that one should not eat the same foods every day as it increases the chances of developing an intolerance; the limit should be five times a week. To my mind, gut, and palette, that works!

I do miss grains. Oatmeal and quinoa were mainstays in my past life, with occasional brown rice—though cauliflower rice is a great substitute! I loved my steaming bowl of steel cut oats with berries, walnuts, or pumpkin seeds, and maple syrup on a cold winter's morning. That tradition now feels like a distant memory. I miss toast too. My substitute for toast is "Keto Eggless English Muffins" that I make several times a week. There is an expensive keto egg-free bun substitute called Unbun that I invest in to make open-faced sandwiches or for hamburgers. There are many keto bread recipes, but most call for a crazy number of eggs. When using "flax eggs" or "chia eggs", you're limited to no more than two or three before the integrity of the baked good is compromised.

A solid chunk of my day revolves around food preparation and I also practice intermittent fasting, aiming for a fourteen to sixteen hour fasting window. Some days it is easier than others. I aim to minimize the amount of processed food I consume to focus on fresh vegetables or frozen organic fruit. I am disciplined without being obsessed, as I have never been a fan of regimented diets. At this time, at least for me it is a no-brainer, when given the option of healing my brain tumour, or indulging in whatever the heck I want, there is no other choice for me. I am here for the long run!

Self-care and Vitamin N

The majority of friends and family that I have spoken with since my diagnosis have wrestled most with the fact that I ever got cancer to begin with. Renowned for the high priority I have placed on my overall health and wellbeing, I can't blame them for feeling that way. But never once have I asked, "Why me?" In reality, I am more apt to ask, "Why not me?" I have such a diverse knowledge base and seemingly random skills that I now understand why I spent so many years acquiring them: to heal myself—mind, body, and spirit.

Through the autumn of 2019 and into the winter, I maintained certain essential self-care practices that I believe have saved me. First and foremost, getting out into nature on a daily basis—to get my daily dose of Vitamin 'N'—continues to be a non-negotiable. No matter the temperature, I get out with Tillie, for at least a half hour to two hours a day, depending on the weather. It is easy to do where we live, as we're a stone's throw from a wooded trail and a ten-minute walk to another trail that winds around a small lake. Plus, there are so many other options, especially when lakes are frozen!

I continue to practice hydrotherapy all year round: taking short but intensely cold showers several days a week, after using a dry brush to massage my skin followed by the application and massage of oil to 'insulate' prior to hopping into the shower. I adapted the Ayurvedic tradition of oil massage called Abhyanga, as I do not massage the oil into my scalp as is done traditionally. I wear a pair of spandex shorts that cover most of my thighs so as to not negatively impact the calcium/magnesium balance in my body, which according to yogic wisdom is traditionally said to be regulated in the thighs. It's not meant to be a long shower though one can build tolerance. I typically max out at three and a half minutes. Some mornings, I will take a normal warm shower and then turn the faucet to cold in the last minute or two, rubbing my skin vigorously until it is pink. It is invigorating. In the summer, when we are at our cabin, "SoLaCe", I'll go skinny-dipping in our lake first thing in the morning; typically, it's just me, the ducks, and the loons! Tillie does not typically join me early in the morning, and Robert most definitely does not.

Another, more soothing self-care practice that has really helped me is taking a very warm Epsom salts bath with essential oils in the evening a few times a week during autumn, winter, and spring. Some days twenty minutes feels sufficient; other days the water is cool by the time I lift myself out. Every now and again, I have flashbacks to my grand mal seizure in the tub, and the struggle that ensued in the effort to lift myself out. I marvel at how much things have changed in one year.

I continue to incorporate essential oils into my everyday routine. I still diffuse the "brain cancer protocol" (fifteen drops frankincense, six drops cloves, three times a day) as I have diffusers in just about every room in our condo! As well, I am still applying the roller tube of the brain tumour blend of frankincense, clove, and myrrh. For headaches, which have never been debilitating like they were in early 2019, I massage peppermint oil at my temples and on the back of my neck. It is strong, so it only takes a drop or two, and I wash my hands immediately after so as to not mistakenly get my fingers near my eyes.

I have almost reached "pill fatigue" with the number of my daily supplements. But they are really helping me stay healthy, so I'm refining and even adding to my daily schedule as the months progress. In the warmer months, I consume organic wheat grass powder in water twice a day. A couple of issues that I have had to work through as I detox my body from the concurrent radiation/chemo, the further six rounds of chemo, and the adjustment to the ketogenic diet are muscle spasms and constipation. It took some juggling to figure out what would resolve the former, but ensuring my magnesium stores are high enough as well as my calcium and potassium balance seem to have resolved that irritating issue for the most part. I still get them on occasion, particularly if I have consumed more than three litres of liquid that day. Most folks struggle to consume sufficient water on a daily basis. I have the opposite struggle: tending to over-saturate my cells. For my constipation, I learned that this is a common problem for those following the keto diet, and began to supplement with stirring a teaspoon of psyllium husk into a glass of water, increasing my daily intake of fibre, as well as introducing the gentle, tonifying Ayurvedic supplement called Triphala, which I take at night with a glass of warm water. I take liquid magnesium bis-glycinate at night to what is called "bowel tolerance" before bed to relax. Works like magic!

Over the winter, I did seventeen one-hour rounds in an infrared sauna at Juniper Health to help detox. I resumed the IV Vitamin C in June on my return from Edmonton and my MRI at the end of May.

Additionally, I continue to meditate daily, using various styles and approaches to the practice which include: Gratitude—which includes journaling before bed a minimum of three things for which I'm grateful each day, Lovingkindness/Metta, Mindfulness, breath work and Kundalini Meditations (usually a single meditation for forty days). Yoga remains an almost daily practice, usually Kundalini but increasingly, various styles of Hatha. Several times a week I set up in a restorative yoga posture for a minimum of thirty minutes in the mid-afternoon. A friend referred me to free "Yoqi" (Yoga and Qigong) videos on YouTube with a beautiful soul named Marissa in the summer of 2019. In recent months, I have been developing a far more regular practice of Qigong as I have been quite drawn to this as a practice. Listening to my body to discover what it needs is essential. I tweak my daily routine accordingly.

Next Level Healing

Through the winter and early spring, I have been feeling blocked in my sacral chakra as well as my throat chakra. My creative artistic expression took a nosedive after completing two paintings in the autumn. I've been quite consumed with writing this memoir, which I acknowledge is certainly a creative endeavour: just not what I am accustomed to. I booked a session with Jillian to help me resolve these blocks at the end of November and as usual, there were several topics to be worked through. I was encouraged to connect with the Elements once more: Wind to filter, Water to purify, Earth to ground, Sound to permeate, Light to expand, and Metal to alchemize all of the shifts. The Record Keepers explained that I had created a boundary whereby I had deemed myself not worthy of Divine Mother's love; thus I was asked to reconnect to all mothers in all lifetimes to release the shame. Specifically, my homework was to chant "Ma", representing the Divine Mother, as well as a traditional Kundalini mantra known as "Laya Yoga", visualizing the serpent energy of the Kundalini winding up my spine from the root up and out of my crown chakra to connect to my forces of creation.

Using Light Languages, the Record Keepers cleared the trauma stored in my sexual organs and I was invited to visualize my womb as a twenty-four-karat golden egg as they used the element of water to cleanse and clear the blockages. I was to imagine being held in the flow of the waters by the Mother of All Divine Beings.

The Record Keepers make a point of working on my brain in each session and are always excited to do so. This time, Jillian mentioned that there was a vast amount of golden white light being beamed directly at the mass, with all energy sent to reduce it in size. Jillian described the image of insects coming in and consuming tiny pieces of my tumour, which was a bit unnerving, but I focused on their consumption of my tumour. I was exhausted and in need of hydration and sleep after this session concluded.

Hard Lesson Learned

I received an energetic and nervous system shock in late November, while participating in the annual "White Tantric Yoga" course in Vancouver. Within the tradition of Kundalini Yoga as taught by Yogi Bhajan™, there is a powerful channelled meditative practice called "White Tantric Yoga", held once a year in various locations around the world. There are only four places in Canada that hold the event: Vancouver, Toronto, Ottawa, and Montreal. It is an intense full day of practice, and not for the faint of heart. It is meant to enable one to break through subconscious blocks in short order. As a prerequisite to gaining full certification within the tradition of Kundalini Yoga as taught by Yogi Bhajan™, I had agreed to accompany my sister-in-law, Kathy, to be her partner. I was not new to the practice, as I had done it as part of my teacher's certification in Toronto in 2011 as well as for five excruciating days at the annual ten-day Summer Solstice Celebration in the Jemez Mountains of New Mexico in 2014. I say excruciating not only because it was five straight days of White Tantric Yoga, but that was the year that I had unknowingly but painfully herniated several discs in my lumbar spine but hadn't yet had an MRI to confirm the injury until August.

I flew down to Vancouver on Friday, November 22nd. After taking the SkyTrain and bus to my Airbnb, I spent the sunny autumn day walking, window shopping, and enjoying some lunch, thrilled to be out of the snow at home. Kathy, Rosie, and Margo had made previous plans for the day, but picked me up on their way home, so that we could enjoy dinner at Margo's together. We were all quite fatigued from our respective full days, so I departed soon after the deliciously wholesome dinner. They retrieved me the next morning and we arrived at an already packed hall of almost two hundred yogis dressed in the requisite white clothing. Due to the timing of our arrival, we were left to set up our mats one row away from one of the large speakers mounted on a pedestal. Knowing how loud it was likely to get did not bode well for my wellbeing. I was cranky before we began. One area of respite was that I was facing a wall rather than the large crowd, so I would not be visually over-stimulated. I did catch sight of my soul sister, Erin Sproule, who was attending with her partner, Laurence, so that put me in much better spirits.

A number of people were assigned to circulate up and down the rows in order to monitor the participants; they also served to act as replacements in case someone needed to take an unscheduled break for any reason. Traditionally, once the group has tuned in and has had the format described in great detail, we were led through a series of warm-ups. A facilitator then guided participants through a series of between six and eight kriyas, varying in length up to sixty-two minutes. A kriya consists of a yoga posture (Asana), a hand position (Mudra), breath work (Pranayama), and a mental focus or a mantra. There are breaks between each kriya, and a light vegetarian lunch provided halfway through the day. We were warned in the introduction that this particular workshop series was going to be incredibly challenging. I needed to have taken that warning more seriously than I did.

I overexerted myself that day. I knew I was reaching my edge during the fifth meditation, as the volume and tone of the music and the surrounding chanting interfered with my ability to remain focussed. The break could not have come soon enough. By the time we reached the final meditation, what I needed to have done was excuse myself. But I did not, choosing instead to push myself. The level of difficulty of the arm position combined with the volume of the shrill and outdated organ-based mantra music almost broke me. I had tears streaming down my cheeks and attempted to shield myself from the noise. I did put my hand up for a monitor to come over, but rather than ask her to take my place, instead I let her know I had a brain tumour and asked if they could turn the music down. The man in charge of sound, a cancer survivor himself, made eye contact with me and brought his hands together in Anjali Mudra (prayer position) to slightly bow to me after adjusting the speaker across from me. I certainly appreciated that he did so, but unfortunately, it was not sufficient. I barely made it through and couldn't wait to get out of there. I had agreed to go to dinner with Erin, Laurence, and a few of their yoga friends. It was not a wise decision because I was emotionally drained and thus not great company. I was feeling entirely spent by the time I caught a cab back to my Airbnb.

Once more, I needed to be smacked on the head to learn my lesson. I was a wreck in the days that followed and quite jittery due to the overactivation of my nervous system, resulting in a state of functional freeze, just to get myself safely home the next day. I did a lot of journalling and crying which helped to an extent. It took at least two weeks to comfortably return to a more regulated state of being. I even broke down in tears at the end of my Monday lunch hour meditation class, after one of my caring and intuitive students had inquired about my White Tantric experience, having sensed that something was awry. They all showed huge compassion and we exchanged warm hugs to help ground me.

What helped even more was my late November session with Jillian, who acknowledged the jolt that my nervous system had received. She picked up on it as I answered my phone because my voice was tremulous, as it had been since Saturday night after the White Tantric experience wrapped up. I was given a Tibetan Tantric tool to practice that allows for immediate restoration of the nervous system and the Vagus nerve through controlled breathing. When agitated, I was to visualize a tub filled with water, recognize that the water is me and imagine that my root chakra is the plug in the tub. I was to pull the plug to allow the water to drain back into the earth. Given all the time I spend in the tub, that was an easy visualization process.

As Jillian began to channel the Light Languages, I gave in to an undeniable urge to silently wail, barely able to breathe my grief was so deep, allowing whatever needed to be released to come up and out. So much energetic weight lifted! Once I composed myself, Jillian asked me to repeat the following statements: "I, Maureen Ann Tonge, release all shame, all levels of programs designed to keep me small. I am free to be who I am meant to be. I embrace all self-judgments with love."

139

Additionally, the Record Keepers recognized that my sensitivity to frequencies had expanded significantly: to words and sounds in particular. I was encouraged to become far more discerning regarding my exposure to media like television, radio, and internet; if a frequency was aggravating to me, I was to remove myself from it. Further, I was to become more cognizant of my own choice of words because words have power and frequency. Admittedly, I curse a lot less than I used to! They suggested that I invest in a water purification system that removes chlorine and other "human-added chemicals", as well as alkalizing and re-mineralizing the water. I was also to begin a practice of chanting "Sat Nam" over my food before consuming and to develop a practice of praying more. I was guided to invest in tools that help to neutralize geomagnetic frequencies, electromagnetic radiation (EMR) and fields (EMF). Since doing so, I definitely feel more grounded; putting my phone on flight mode at night and not having it in the bedroom helps too. I also leave the room when my husband's choice of television shows over-activates my nervous system.

Near the end of this session, I was informed by the Record Keepers through Jillian, that I was ready for the next level. I was not entirely sure what that meant, except to reflect on the metaphor of peeling the layers of the onion. We would be going deeper still in our remaining sessions over the winter and into spring.

My Winter of (Dis)Content

There were two main events in December: early in the month, I flew down to Edmonton to meet Kirsten who would accompany me to my MRI and to the Outpatient Exam where we would receive the results of my exam. The second event was with my husband: for the first time in twenty years, we would be spending Christmas with members of his family in Manitoba. Given how brutally cold it was in Yellowknife, we counted the days until we could fly somewhere marginally milder. Robert's sister, Thecla, and her husband, Jeff, live approximately ninety minutes northeast of Winnipeg, which is often referred to as "Winterpeg". Despite the nickname, Christmas was forecast to be mild in Winnipeg and surrounding areas.

Robert was reluctant to stay behind in Yellowknife in early December; but he wasn't able to get the time off work to join us in Edmonton. I assured him that Kirst and I were very excited at the prospect of spending three and a half days together for some twinnie time in Edmonton, and that I would keep in regular contact, particularly once I received the results.

My MRI was at 3:30 that afternoon, so we had ample time to eat and rest a bit before walking to the Cross Cancer Institute. The exam was uneventful; in fact, I was so relaxed that I almost dozed off more than once.

I had booked a VAHT session with Bev Ross for the following morning, trusting that the sound-healing experience of the harp would relax me prior to us receiving the results. My VAHT session was fantastic. The sounds of the harp were exactly what I needed for grounding. I floated back to the hotel, having time to grab a bite to eat before walking to CCI. A nurse and a doctor whom we had never seen before met with us. It became readily apparent that the doctor hadn't read my file beyond the most recent MRI results. "Any more seizures?" she asked after introducing herself, followed by "So, you're still taking the anti-seizure medications?" Considering I had never taken any anti-seizure medications and hadn't had any tumour-related pain or seizures since January—which I let her know—she appeared shocked by my unexpected responses.

Grinning widely, she then informed us of the thrilling news: my MRI results illustrated that my tumour remained medically stable, though actually indicated a slight decrease in volume. Once we got a copy of the report, Kirst did the math which revealed that my tumour had shrunk by almost 90% since February 24th! I was then informed that I was being placed on "Surveillance Status" and would no longer have to do monthly blood work; and that my MRIs would be every three months instead of every two. Yay! We contacted our family immediately to share the news. I sent Robert a text showing a flexed bicep and heart emojis so that he would know the results were positive, as he was in a workshop while we were in my exam. He called as soon as he could to get the details, saying, "obviously, whatever you are doing is working!" He was relieved as he admitted to being tied up in an anxious knot before this great news.

Prior to my appointment, we had arranged to meet my dear friend and former condo neighbour, Dawn Curtis, later that afternoon to walk with her dog, Hank, neither of whom I'd seen since they moved south from Yellowknife in September. As Kirst and I buoyantly bopped back to the hotel, I texted Dawn to ask her to swing by with Hank to pick us up, as the four of us were heading to William Hawrelak Park so that Hank could be off-leash as we walked the various wooded trails. They arrived with Hank's head hanging out the wide open back window. He was wiggly with happiness to see his "auntie" again. Meeting Kirst— who is a confirmed dog magnet—was a treat for both, as she hopped in the backseat to snuggle with Hanky Panky, as I have dubbed this love bug.

It was a lovely late autumn afternoon, and the fresh air crisply enlivening. We walked for a while before making our way back to the vehicle to drive to Dawn's new condo on the northwest edge of downtown Edmonton. We had made dinner reservations for 6:00 pm at Pampa Brazilian Steakhouse, an easy walk from Dawn's place. All three of us ate our fill, but I ate something that didn't agree with me and had an unhappy belly for the rest of the evening. Dawn drove us back to the hotel and we said our goodbyes. It was that evening that Kirst shared with me what the neurosurgeon had predicted regarding my prognosis. Funnily enough, I learned that Robert thought I knew all along, which is why he never brought it up! I had been oblivious, and gratefully so.

As often happens when one experiences such wonderful highs, there is the inevitable polarity of the lows. With the increasingly short and brutally cold days and long dark nights, I experienced quite a few mood swings, and it became, for a time, a challenge for me to remain focused on the blessings in my life. I was irritable and short-tempered with my husband, and he with me. The middle part of December was a tough month to handle.

Fortunately, I was given an opportunity to snap out of my funk, as I was invited to take part in a special segment of the local CBC North's show, *Trail's End*, which was focused on gratitude. I was touched to have been asked to share my miraculous story with the northern audience. Speaking and sharing was the medicine I needed to shift my Scrooge-like mentality. After that well-received interview, I felt like I had found my holiday spirit.

Ho-Ho-Holidays

It felt quite surreal not to have put up any Christmas decorations in our condo, though one day Robert brought home a tiny potted tree of some sort that we put in the centre of our dining table. The tree lasted for months, though its tiny branches would not tolerate weight of any kind, so decorating it was out of the question. We had good friends willing to take in Tillie for the holidays along with their two pooches, so we were reassured that she would be well-loved while we were in Manitoba. Our flight departed dark and early on Winter Solstice and we landed safely in Winnipeg to be greeted by my sister-in-law and brother-in-law.

It was the first time ever that Robert and I visited the Melnicks at the same time.

Robert and I were gifted the basement, which had a wonderfully open space for me to do my daily yoga and meditation. It also allowed me to escape when I needed to, which I was grateful that Thecla recognized I would need. When all the Melnicks are together, as they were on Christmas Eve, they are a joyfully boisterous bunch. I did make my way downstairs before dinner while the others took up an outdoor street hockey game. I am told that Robert impressed all with his rusty but still evident prowess, scoring several goals.

One of their girls generously gifted me a one-hour massage early into our trip, as Thecla has a massage table set up under a small loft on their second floor. The girl has strong hands!

Robert and I had decided not to exchange gifts, electing instead to use the trip as our mutual gift. Thecla would not hear of us not having stockings, however, and thoughtfully stuffed one for each of us so that we could join them on Christmas morning. We had gotten each of them a small gift as well.

We had two Christmas dinners: the first with the larger Melnick family on Christmas Eve, and a second with just the seven of us on Christmas Day. I took on the task of making a Keto Pecan Pie, which I had never made before. Though I could have baked it for five minutes less, it was pretty darn tasty!

Jeff and Thecla have an outdoor sauna, which the four older adults enjoyed a couple of times. There was not enough snow to roll in, so Jeff hooked up the hose, which we used to douse ourselves with ice cold water before returning to the steamy sauna. Jeff was a big fan of scooping water over the hot rocks on top of the wood stove. I found it to be way too much steam, so left the sauna several times to gulp cooler air.

Everyone in that house was into jigsaw puzzles except me as I have zero patience for them. It was fascinating for me to watch their focused attention on assembling two one-thousand-piece puzzles and one three-thousand-piece puzzle in the six days that we were there. We balanced our days with reading, napping, and by getting out to hike or walk in the rural area where they live right on the Winnipeg River. Thecla and I took one day to drive to Pinawa, across the bridge, to go ice skating on an outdoor community rink. I felt like a calf learning how to walk for the first several minutes, but somehow managed to stay upright. Afterward, we hiked the short distance to the dam. I had only seen it in summer before, so to see how the rushing water froze and created ice sculptures on some of the nearby trees was beautiful.

Cold Shower at the Melnicks in Manitoba

Time flew, and we reluctantly packed up the morning of December 27th. Thecla stayed home with the girls while Jeff drove Robert and me to the airport. I sat in the back as Robert and Jeff spent the entire time gabbing enthusiastically in the front seat. I had a happy heart, as I do not think I had ever seen my husband talk that much. I got a kick out of Robert's quizzing Jeff on the price of lots and homes in the area. We

145

already decided to retire in Yellowknife but given the much lower cost of living in Manitoba, I think his mental wheels got turning. I had to remind him that the mosquitos are often worse there than where we live!

Robert departed the morning after we returned, as he was taking three of his adult children to the cabin. In his absence, I had booked an infrared sauna appointment for Saturday afternoon, a session with Jillian the evening of the 30th, and a noon-hour New Year's Eve Intention-Setting and Healing Gong session at Collective Soul Space, which was by donation. Over $300 was raised for the Brain Tumour Foundation of Canada that noon hour.

To say that my session with Jillian was powerful would not do it justice. Much of the session revolved around healing my in-utero relationship with my twinnie. Now, as an adult, I needed to stop taking on my sister's energy as it was at this point subconsciously ingrained to do so. To recognize the next level of self-worthiness, I was invited to recite the following vow: "I, Maureen Ann Tonge, with every cell of my being, stand tall as a beacon of light, as one who shows the way: embracing all of my gifts so that others can see their own divinity within themselves. I choose ME so they can choose them. I am not responsible for others. I am not responsible for processing other people's energies. God loves me. I love God. God loves everyone else. I am not God." After my recitation, somewhat hilariously, the Record Keepers asked: "Why isn't fighting terminal cancer enough?" Point taken. I have revisited that question numerous times since.

My homework involved Mirror Work: gazing into a handheld mirror and speaking aloud phrases revolving around self-worthiness. Encouraged to give up the pattern of trying to fit in and be "normal", I was to allow my gifts and light to shine. When it came time to work on my brain tumour, I was to visualize my head bathed in golden light and picture one thousand lasers and energy obliterating the tumour. It was an intense experience of Light Languages, as quite literally the electricity kept zapping, causing my headphones to cut out repeatedly.

As we wrapped up the session with the Record Keepers, Jillian shared that whenever I felt the undertow of starting to take on and absorb the energy of one of my sisters, I was to invite the "Little Maureen" to sit on my lap and remind her that she is loved and has everything she needs inside of her. She does not have to fix anyone else for them to love her. It was also recommended that I acquire a weighted blanket as it is very soothing for the nervous system, which I did.

Invalid Expiry Date

Robert returned on the 31st to drop off the kids and retrieve me and Tillie so that we could spend New Year's Eve at the cabin. My predicted "expiry date" came and went as we eased our way through the remaining hours of 2019. Tillie joined me on the two-kilometre hike in: I was on snowshoes, and Robert snowmobiled with the food. He had stoked the woodstove as fully as possible prior to departing with the kids, so the cabin was merely cool as opposed to freezing when we arrived as dusk was settling in the afternoon. It was a peaceful, relaxing, and relatively balmy New Year's Eve at "SoLaCe", spent listening to CBC Radio's New Year's Eve programming as we cooked dinner. Afterward, I insisted that we each make a list of things for which we were grateful in 2019. Foremost on the list was my still being present and progressively healing. With the short and dark days, we were in bed by 9:00 or 10:00 pm. Robert worked on a puzzle and I read, meditated, and practiced yoga the next day followed by a hearty brunch. We were fortunate that temperatures were inordinately mild as the daytime temps hovered in the negative mid-teens, which made getting outside much more palatable.

Mom and Dad arrived in Yellowknife to temperatures of -38C. In the time they spent with us in our small condo, I don't think the temperature rose above -30C. They were able to witness a spectacular show of the Aurora Borealis their first night in town from the warm comfort of our dining and living room, looking out the picture windows with all the lights turned off. We had given them the master suite so they would have ready access to the ensuite bathroom in the middle of the night. They did, however, have to be careful not to trip over Tillie, who had developed the tricky habit of sleeping in the entryway to the bathroom. Tillie whined less during their stay. The previous January, when my symptoms were dramatically worsening, she had developed the highly irritating habit of almost incessant whining. I recognize now that she is so highly sensitive, she had undoubtedly picked up on my illness and appeared helpless in her concern. I'll admit to having an ulterior motive for putting my parents in the master bedroom: it gave me my own space to practice my daily yoga and meditation, as Robert and I slept on the Murphy bed.

We hosted the friends with whom Mom and Dad had stayed in the summer when they were up for Grad, Jacqueline and Roger, for a Happy Hour visit Saturday afternoon as part of Mom's early birthday celebration. Sunday I was hosting a Full Moon Meditation with Healing Gong on Mom's actual birthday, which is why we decided to have the birthday dinner the night before.

Mom had never experienced the Full Moon Meditation with Healing Gong before and was excited to do so. It was a solid turnout of participants and I introduced the group to my mama, mentioning that it was her birthday. We all sang "Happy Birthday" to her before beginning the meditation, which made her blush. She enjoyed the meditations very much, though struggled with voice projection during the mantra recitations. That was not at all surprising to me, as she has struggled with her fifth (throat) chakra, having experienced several related health issues, such as thyroid cancer. As for the healing gong, she found it too loud at times despite being set up at the back of the room. I totally understood how and why that would be her initial experience. It took me several experiences of the gong to acclimate to the sound vibrations. Overall, what she loved most was to see me in action and being obviously well-loved by those in attendance.

For the final two days of my parents' visit, we were able to drive on the recently opened ice road, an almost seven-kilometer shortcut linking Yellowknife to the indigenous community of Dettah across

Yellowknife Bay. It had been years since they had travelled on it, and it was a clear and cold winter's afternoon when we ventured out. Being the fun-loving trooper she is, Mom laid down and moved her arms to create a snow angel when we stopped for the requisite photo op. Dad would have as well, but his back and right leg sciatic issues were such that he feared not being able to get up again. We cut him some slack.

As a belated Christmas gift for Mom and Dad, I had booked them appointments: for Mom, a pedicure at my favourite spa in Yellowknife, Etandah, and for Dad, an acupuncture appointment with William. Dad was moving remarkably better after his session, which allowed for his long flight back to Ottawa to be more comfortable. When I picked Mom up at noon, she was thrilled with her toes, having selected a beautiful deep blue hue. We had time for lunch before I took them to the airport. Getting them checked through was smooth and it was with sadness mixed with huge love and gratitude that we said goodbye. It felt strange not having already made plans to see one another again.

Back to Routine

The three-week cold snap broke by the third week of January, and we were able to get out to the cabin by the last weekend of the month. It still took several hours for the cabin to warm up, but we kept busy with outdoor tasks such a shovelling the decks, the tipi, and moving our old propane fridge into the toboggan. Robert augured a hole in the ice for water; the ice was at least two feet thick but a Christmas present from a few years back was a rechargeable battery-operated ice auger that works like a dream. Once the cabin warmed up, we spent much of our time reading in front of the woodstove, napping, and eating well.

When we returned home, I maintained my routines as Robert went on his two regularly scheduled annual "boys' trips": a long weekend in Montreal to catch a couple of Canadiens hockey games followed by five days in Palm Springs. We were filled with relief as we reflected on how different this year's trips were compared to last year. He was able to relax and thoroughly enjoy bonding with his buddies, while I took advantage of the quiet, sleeping diagonally on our king-sized bed and not once turning on the television.

In the interest of continuing education, I had signed up to do a three-day Yoga Tune-up™ training being held mid-February. We began at the highly reasonable hour of 10:00 am but would then go until 6:00 or sometimes 7:00 pm. It was not physically challenging; however, the mental stimulation of absorbing so much information combined with the fluorescent lighting in the studio was utterly draining. By the time we wrapped up the training on Sunday evening, Robert forbade me to commit to anything like that again for the foreseeable future. It was just too much in the way of energy expenditure for me. That said, I love the practice of using the Yoga Tune-up™ balls for self-massage, and still use them daily.

I have become rather addicted to listening to audiobooks on Audible. Some of my faves in February were *Rising Strong* by Brene Brown, and *Light is the New Black* by Rebecca Campbell.

As the anniversary of my being medivaced to Edmonton approached, I could not help but marvel at my miraculous healing. Coincidentally, my next scheduled MRI and follow-up Outpatient Exam was taking place almost a year to the day of my diagnosis, on February 26th and 27th.

Chapter 13

Setbacks and Recommitments

MY FEBRUARY MRI results were somewhat concerning. Though still considered medically stable, there appeared on the scan to be something medical personnel referred to as a "hyper-intensity". They thought it might have been on the December scan as well, but it was more obvious in February. It was something to keep an eye on, but the doctors didn't appear overly concerned about it at the time. I was informed that my follow-up MRI would be in May, likely right after my birthday. At that point, I hadn't been experiencing any major symptoms except the pressure I was feeling between my temples, especially when in meditation and focusing my gaze at the third eye, said to stimulate the pituitary and pineal glands. Periodic light-headedness arose, but since I struggle with orthostatic hypotension and low blood pressure on a good day, it was nothing I concerned myself with. The pressure between my temples continued to build, so much so that I informed my family doctor. Plus, I booked an appointment with a local massage therapist who specializes in cranio-sacral therapy and energy healing in early March. She chalked it up to too shallow breathing as I relaxed into my meditations. But despite making conscious efforts to fill into the lower lobes of my lungs, the pressure in my temples only temporarily lessened.

Hindsight 2.0

In March, I was well over halfway through a forty-day Kundalini Yoga practice called the "Sahibi Kriya to Master Your Domain"; it includes a lot of powerful mouth breathing and leg lifts. As is expected, some days were easier than others to meet the challenge of the leg lifts and vigorous breathwork. I had also committed to redoing the "Smart Body, Smart Mind" twelve-week online course with nervous system dysregulation expert, Irene Lyon and her team, which started in mid-March. I was still teaching yoga and meditation classes up until the pandemic shut down my teaching spaces in mid-March. There was more than enough on my plate trying to keep up with the weekly training and Q and A calls for the ten-module SBSM course, though we were consistently reminded to pace ourselves and to not rush the process. I followed that advice, and as a result still have a good deal of the final two modules to get through. Additionally, I began the "Heroic Heart" forty-day meditation practice with the Life Force Academy that began on Good Friday. I never felt like I connected with that particular meditation, which involved taking on the suffering of others, similar to the Buddhist practice of Tonglen. As an empath, I struggled. Thus, in hindsight, I needed to have let go of that commitment without apology. But some habits are so hard to break, and I am no quitter.

I had just returned home from the cabin on April 19th to several missed calls from Kirsten, who finally left a voicemail where she shared the devastating news of a childhood friend being gunned down outside her home in Portapique, Nova Scotia the previous night. I was inconsolable. I soon learned that Lis was one of twenty-two innocent victims in what was Canada's worst mass murder in recorded history. Our families had grown up together in our hometown's United Church and we had kept in sporadic contact over the years since adulthood. Notably, Lis had reached out to me the previous spring when I was in Edmonton for my treatments and we exchanged a number of messages before resuming a less regular but still love-filled connection on Facebook. Lis and I shared our strong spiritual beliefs in angels, guides, and other beings. She was in a really great head and heart space when she was viciously murdered by a madman. Though an absolutely devastating loss to all who knew her, I'm certain that Lis has joined her brother in sharing their angelic light with their remaining family members.

As the pandemic began its global rampage, the chief medical officer shut down our borders to visitors and non-NWT residents.

I did my best to shelter myself from the drone of the same tragic news stories being repeated ad nauseum on CBC Radio and television. This is a much easier task when we spend time at our cabin, which is entirely off-grid in the winter and spring, save CBC North radio, which I only allow on for limited periods of time.

In May, I was still practicing yoga on a daily basis, but was noticing my mental capacity and physical stamina were suffering as I had developed some internal shakiness. My sleep continued to be disrupted and dream-filled. I had a growing sense of being unsettled and could not put my finger on what was going on as a heightening low-grade anxiety also took up residence. I committed to participating in an online twenty-one-day Tapping Challenge with Dawson Church, PhD, which I found highly beneficial despite an interesting point in the process when I stopped getting the daily emails at Day sixteen. Fascinatingly, the last session I received access to was called "Tapping into Your Higher Self"; during my recent session with Jillian, the Record Keepers had noted that there was a complete disconnect in the relationship between me and my Higher Self! I elected to repeat that tapping script until I felt like I was establishing a connection. Sure enough, the Universe responded by sending me the remaining of the twenty-one days! I had to laugh.

By mid-May, we could finally host my stepson Jacob and his girlfriend Katie for dinner, which we were thrilled to do. As the date of my next MRI approached, I found myself contemplating the idea of returning to work in some capacity in 2021.

Devastated But Not Defeated

I flew to Calgary, where, Nat picked me up and we drove together to Edmonton. Because of the pandemic, no visitors were allowed in the Cross Cancer Institute; thus, I had to go through the entire process alone—not an experience I ever care to repeat! I did not much mind being alone for the MRI; they were fairly on time getting me in for the scan and it went smoothly.

The following day dawned sunny and full of potential. We had made patio picnic lunch plans with a friend. Later, as we made our way to CCI for my Outpatient Exam, I was relaxed and feeling prepared to receive the results. Nat reminded me that she would be the first person I saw once I received the update and departed the building.

Unwelcome Answers

The pressure I had been experiencing in my temples and the shakiness and mild discombobulation make a lot more sense now! I had an inkling that my results were not as I hoped when the two resident doctors came in and asked, "Has anyone shared any news of your results yet?" They had not, which seemed to dismay them. The male resident gently shared the news: not only has my original tumour started re-growing, I also have three additional lesions on my brain I was stunned by the news: devastated if entirely truthful with myself. They gave me a copy of the imaging, and to see my brain with its foreign and unwelcome growths was traumatizing. It was shocking to see the rapid growth that had taken place since February. I have since learned that is fairly common GBM behaviour. The resident doctors were extremely apologetic at my having to be alone to receive the blow. Meanwhile, Nat suspected something was up because I was taking an inordinate amount of time in the exam room. The doctors explained that they were hoping to put me back on chemo: a different one this time called Etoposide. It can be taken daily without a break and I was booked to return for my next MRI in two months' time. They invited me to call my insurance company to ensure that the chemo drug, administered in pill form, would be covered: thankfully, it is, and the woman I spoke with was wonderfully sympathetic when I shared my news. The doctors spent a good deal of time ensuring I was clear as to what my next steps were with them. I had a brief conversation with Robert, and he promised to call me as soon as he was done with his virtual work meeting. I also called Kirst and asked her to call Mom, Dad, Joce, and Mel. Before I could leave CCI, I needed to get baseline blood work done. It was emotionally agonizing, as all I wanted to do was get the hell out of the building, so I could openly sob and hug Nat. I had to stop myself from fleeing and as Nat and I clung together, we were both wracked with heart-breaking sobs. Thank God I had her to hold me up.

Bless her, once we were checked in, Nat left to go to a grocery store so that we would have some nourishing, healthy food, despite not having an appetite. While Nat was out, I reached out to each of my sisters who by now had heard from Mom and Dad. I called Robert's family as well, sharing my tears with his sisters; I wasn't able to reach his mom, so I left a voicemail, which is not ideal, but it was all I could do.

Sleep was fitful, and no alarm was necessary to wake up, pack up, and make our way to the airport. Nat and I exchanged fierce hugs, more tears, exclamations of our mutual love and adoration, and we parted.

I shed many tears in the days and weeks ahead. I began my chemo on May 29th and most gratefully, the worst of my side effects to date is a perpetual deep fatigue and the gradual shedding of my beloved ringlets. It's most essential for me to recognize when I have hit the wall and need to lie down. I do on a daily basis. I lack physical stamina, which is understandable and something I'm learning to accept. I'm learning the importance of deep listening to what it is that my body truly requires. Currently, my physical practice of yoga has dropped off almost entirely, but not quite. Instead, I am doing a primal dance each morning—often naked (!) to a piece of music on Insight Timer called "Awaken the Kundalini". I am also practicing a hybridized energy balancing routine put together by Donna Eden, which I am thoroughly benefitting from as it's a combination of Qigong and tapping type practices.

I have been journalling a lot; in fact, filled up my gorgeous journal that I received from a friend. After listening to and reading the book, *Love Yourself Like Your Life Depends On It* by Kamal Ravikant, I completed the four exercises detailed in the book. The most potent one for me was writing a list of all of the things that I'd been holding against myself, allowing for any and all emotions to surface, feel them fully, and once I sensed the urgency of the emotions had passed, then to write the words, "I forgive myself" repeatedly until I felt lighter. It worked! I then took the piece of paper down to the rocks below our front patio overlooking Yellowknife Bay and carefully burned the paper. That entire experience shifted something major in me. I experienced a liberation like I had not before. Even Jillian recognized the potency of this one particular exercise for me, which I thought was really cool.

The other exercise that I found almost equal in power and potency was the writing of a vow to myself that I would read aloud at least twice a day: first thing in the morning (even before arising) and before bed at night.

My Vow

"I, Maureen Ann Tonge, vow that from this day forward, I will value, honour, respect, and above all else, LOVE myself, without expectation nor judgment. To accept myself as being human and therefore, not perfect. To show a whole-hearted, enthusiastic, and expressively demonstrative love for myself and my gifts that I have to share with this world. To understand the power that I have within me to fully embody my radiant connection to God's love—the all-encompassing love that never fails nor ever dies. And so it is."

I wrote this while at the cabin early in June, and also received an intuitive "hit" to let Robert know verbally that I had made the full-on whole-hearted commitment to heal and to live. His response? "You better!" Admittedly, I had spent the previous week after receiving the latest results feeling a bit "laissez faire" and "Well, why not see what's waiting for me once I leave this physical body?" After all, I truly have no fear of dying. None. In a conversation with Kirst in early June, she confessed to me, "This feels different" to which I agreed. It does feel different this time. Most days, I am okay with that. My core belief that we have the power within us to heal remains steadfast. I will heal.

My next MRI is July 29th in Edmonton and both Robert and Kirst will be accompanying me; only one of them will be allowed to accompany me during my appointments unless the restrictions are eased. I figure they can arm wrestle to determine the victor! Amazingly and most impressively, my chemo oncologist called me two weeks after my return, after having begun my chemo. It felt more like a conversation among people who genuinely wish to learn and understand more about what the other person had to offer. He was highly impressed with my discipline and commitment not only to the ketogenic diet ("that's no joke!" he shared) explaining the growing scientific evidence in support of its adoption with GBMs; but also my other habits and practices. He had lots of questions, providing acknowledgement of my cold showers, the practice of which he has also adopted, and my mind, body, spirit practices including of course, meditation.

I recommenced my IV therapy sessions of DCA and Poly-MVA at Juniper Health after having phone or Zoom appointments with all three of my naturopathic doctors. Together, they formulated a Plan B for my schedule of supplements, hormone replacement (bioidentical and desiccated thyroid) as well as IVs. By June, I was booked twice weekly, with each session taking at least three hours of being hooked up on a bed to IV. Unfortunately, my DCA dose had to be cut in half because of the neuropathy I experienced in my right arm, hand, leg, and foot. I found myself in the emergency room after my first or second session to get a CT scan after my symptoms did not abate on the drive home from the cabin. I had not linked the numbness and tingling to my IV therapy at that point, despite it being a common side effect of IV DCA. It was not at all painful: more like a limb that had fallen asleep, especially when I lifted my arm, which had been resting on Tillie's head on the drive home. It was then that the ER doctor asked me, "Has anyone ever spoken to you about driving?" Oddly not! I had been driving since August of 2019. She informed me that I could voluntarily take myself off the road or she would be legally obligated to write a letter to the Ministry of Transport. I did not have to be persuaded, as I had my husband drop me off at the ER anyway, no longer at ease with being behind the wheel. Seven hours later, with no sign of having had a seizure, Robert was allowed to take me home from the hospital. I was famished, as I hadn't had much in the way of nourishment prior to going to the hospital. I was given a prescription for Dexamethasone, as the CT scan had indicated that the edema in my brain was now in both hemispheres, not just one-sided as had shown on the MRI just two weeks prior. In my follow-up conversation with my Chemo Oncologist which took place after my trip to the ER, he suggested that I only take a half dose twice a day for a week followed by a half dose once a day for a week of the dexamethasone and then stop entirely.

I do feel like I have had my proverbial wings clipped, but of course I completely understand and wouldn't wish to endanger anyone's life, including my own. Fortunately, I have a cruiser bike that is well-recognized around town as it is "me to a T": lemon-green with a plastic wicker basket attached adorned with a fabric sunflower. It's a blast booting around town, as complete strangers wave and smile as they pass. I am never short of offers for lifts from friends either and of course, my husband has been most gracious about chauffeuring me.

The Gifts of a Terminal Diagnosis

As I adjust to this new reality, I had to wrap my head around how I wished to travel through this slight detour on my healing journey. Early one morning just two days prior to Summer Solstice, I was inspired to journal a list of what I had decided were the "Gifts of a Terminal Diagnosis". They are subject to revision and are based purely on my experience as I cannot and will not speak for anyone else. These ideas are certainly not unique to me. In this age of massive transformation and global shifting, I am but one of many beings inhabiting this glorious planet, with the desire to be open to experiencing these energetic shifts from a place of humility, courage, and grace.

- The recognition that as we know, we grow. We are in charge of our perspective and make the ultimate choice as to what we allow into our environment; when we know better, we have the opportunity to do better.
- We are multi-layered, multi-dimensional beings. As we increase in our awareness, and the awareness of our personal power to

158

control our breath, our mindset, and thus our health, we are better able to open ourselves to our highest potential of who we are. As we peel away the layers—and rather than stuffing things down, we allow ourselves to feel all of the emotions that need to arise—then, as time and repetition of the process allows, we heal. Approaching this from a place of self-love, gentleness, patience, and kindness will be required. Judgment has no place in the healing process, particularly of self.

- Another gift that I experienced through the past year is the importance of being open to receive the gifts of others. To be reminded and to finally accept that I am not aiming for perfection: and that the hundreds of people in my life, by and large truly wish to be of service and express their love for me.

- Quantum science tells us that wherever you bring your attention to causes the object of your attention to change. As we are into crazy mosquito season here in the NWT, I have noticed that the volume of their sound and number seem to increase as I am awoken in the early morning hours by the buzzing. Sleeping with a bug jacket on and the sheet pulled up over my head—and possibly wearing earplugs are key tricks to maintaining sanity. If I open the curtain, I quickly pick up on the reality that though my screen may be covered by the swarm of the bloodthirsty critters, there is in reality only one or two that have somehow made it upstairs into the loft of our cabin. There is a gift in shedding light on the reality of one's current situation.

- One of the biggest gifts—aside from the full-on trust that we have the ability to heal ourselves from whatever dis-ease we are experiencing—is my non-negotiable practice of gratitude. Not a day goes by without my contributing to my Gratitude Journal. The act of forgiving myself and writing my vow was hugely healing and was a necessary process: truly a gift of self-love and acceptance.

- As I am presented with a challenge, learning to identify the lesson within is key to my soul's evolution. Otherwise, and as was the pattern in my life, the lesson repeats and becomes progressively more serious in nature until it is learned. I am finally paying full attention and have experienced life-changing affirmation, no matter the outcome.

Perhaps the greatest gift of hindsight is that it is 20/20. With this crazy year of upheaval on all levels: environmental, racial, socio-economic, and political, we are being given the opportunity to heal generational wounds, both personally and within our communities and the world at large. No more denial. It is time.

THE END

Getting ready to kayak on Saturday, June 27ᵗʰ in the Virtual Brain Tumour Foundation "Walk" 2020 (photo credit: Robert Charpentier)

About the Author

B ORN IN NEW Brunswick, Maureen made her second home in Yellowknife, NWT where she spent 28 years teaching at a local high school. Her passion for Kundalini yoga offered connections around the world. Maureen's spirituality and strong beliefs in integrative energetic healing led her through a miraculous journey. Maureen made her final transition on October 5, 2020 at home surrounded by her loving family.

PGIL2020USA